ISSUES THAT CONCERN YOU

Endangered
Species

Cynthia A. Bily, *Book Editor*

GREENHAVEN PRESS
A part of Gale, Cengage Learning

GALE
CENGAGE Learning

Detroit • New York • San Francisco • New Haven, Conn • Waterville, Maine • London

Christine Nasso, *Publisher*
Elizabeth Des Chenes, *Managing Editor*

© 2010 Greenhaven Press, a part of Gale, Cengage Learning

Gale and Greenhaven Press are registered trademarks used herein under license.

For more information, contact:
Greenhaven Press
27500 Drake Rd.
Farmington Hills, MI 48331-3535
Or you can visit our Internet site at gale.cengage.com

For product information and technology assistance, contact us at

Gale Customer Support, 1-800-877-4253
For permission to use material from this text or product, submit all requests online at www.cengage.com/permissions

Further permissions questions can be e-mailed to permissionrequest@cengage.com

Articles in Greenhaven Press anthologies are often edited for length to meet page requirements. In addition, original titles of these works are changed to clearly present the main thesis and to explicitly indicate the author's opinion. Every effort is made to ensure that Greenhaven Press accurately reflects the original intent of the authors. Every effort has been made to trace the owners of copyrighted material.

Image copyright rm, 2010. Used under license from Shutterstock.com.

LIBRARY OF CONGRESS CATALOGING-IN-PUBLICATION DATA

Endangered species / Cynthia A. Bily, book editor.
    p. cm. -- (Issues that concern you)
  Includes bibliographical references and index.
  ISBN 978-0-7377-4953-3 (hardcover)
  1. Endangered species--Juvenile literature. I. Bily, Cynthia A.
  QH75.E645 2010
  333.95'22--dc22

                                                            2010000085

Printed in the United States of America
1 2 3 4 5 6 7 14 13 12 11 10

CONTENTS

One of the most endangered mammals in the world is the little-known black-footed ferret (*Mustela nigripes*), a beautiful sleek creature related to the weasel, skunk, mink, and other animals of the mustelid family. A nocturnal animal about eighteen to twenty-four inches long, the black-footed ferret lives in the native grasslands of the Great Plains—a habitat that is quickly disappearing.

The black-footed ferret disappeared completely from Canada and was added to the federal list of endangered species in the United States in 1967. In the 1980s, biologists captured the last eighteen wild black-footed ferrets in North America and began breeding them in captivity; the estimated seven hundred ferrets that live on the Great Plains now are the descendants of those captive-bred animals. Every year, some 350 to 450 ferret babies, called kits, are born in zoos and refuges, and about 200 of them are introduced into the wild.

Black-footed ferrets have been preyed upon by coyotes, golden eagles, and other animals, and they have also been ravaged by a plague that spread rapidly and greatly reduced their numbers. But the greatest threat they face today is that the region is running out of their favorite food—the black-tailed prairie dog (*Cynomys ludovicianus*). For thousands of years the two species have shared the same habitat. Prairie dogs live in complicated systems of tunnels; the ferrets use these tunnels for shelter, and they eat prairie dogs. In the past this was a good strategy—prairie dogs were plentiful, and eating them kept black-footed ferrets thriving without threatening the prairie dogs' numbers.

But today the ferrets' existence is more complicated. Prairie dogs are disappearing, and the biggest reason is that they are considered pests by the farmers and ranchers who earn their living on the Great Plains. For generations these farmers and ranchers have been killing as many prairie dogs as they can, because the prairie dogs damage crops around their burrows and eat the food that would otherwise be available for cattle to eat. For decades the myth that cattle trip and break their legs in prairie dog burrows has also persisted, but Lindsey Sterling of the Prairie Dog Coalition claims in an article in the July/August 2004 issue of *E Magazine*, "After years of asking ranchers this question, we have found not one example."

Nevertheless, prairie dogs are not welcome on the Great Plains, and the Wildlife Hunters Association of Colorado, for-

For thousands of years black-footed ferrets (left) and their favorite food, prairie dogs (right), have occupied the same habitat. Farmers' continuing destruction of the prairie dog thus threatens the existence of the ferret.

merly known as the "Varmint Militia," sponsors guided prairie dog shoots every year. Its Web site (www.wildlifehunters.com) reports that by 1998 the group's Shoot Outs had "brought the number of trespassers (prairie devils) executed to over 10,000." Recently, a new weapon has been brought to the fight against prairie dogs—one that is far more dangerous to the ferrets. Landowners are killing prairie dogs with poison.

Two poisons approved by the federal Environmental Protection Agency (EPA), Rozol and Kaput-D, are now in widespread use against prairie dogs. The poisons are slow acting, so prairie dogs weaken and die over a period of weeks, making them easy prey for the animals that feed on them. And because the poison lingers in the animals' bodies, predators that eat them become poisoned themselves. Ron Klataske, executive director of Audubon of Kansas, observed in a 2009 press release that several threatened species are affected: "Secondary poisoning with Rozol is a threat to swift foxes, American badgers, ferruginous hawks, golden and bald eagles that frequently feed on prairie dogs in the Great Plains. Black-footed ferrets rely almost exclusively on prairie dogs for food."

Audubon of Kansas teamed up with Defenders of Wildlife in September 2009 to sue the EPA over its approval of the poisons. Supporting their efforts against the EPA, a federal agency, was another federal agency, the U.S. Fish and Wildlife Service, which officially requested the EPA withdraw its approval for these pesticides to be used on black-tailed prairie dogs.

The fate of the black-footed ferret thus rests in the hands of a large number of players. Farmers and ranch owners want to make the best use of their land, and prairie dogs interfere with their ability to earn a good living from their hard work. They are happy to eliminate prairie dogs—the ferrets' main source of food—to protect their livelihood. Environmentalists hoping to rescue the endangered black-footed ferret find themselves at odds with these landowners. Two federal agencies are in disagreement over the best course for managing the Great Plains. But all the people involved place a high value on the outdoors and the animals that live there.

Understanding the conflicts between private landowners and environmentalists is just one of the issues related to endangered species. Authors in this anthology examine the balance between maintaining biological diversity and sustaining economic vitality. In addition, the volume contains several appendixes to help the reader understand and explore the topic, including a thorough bibliography and a list of organizations to contact for further information. The appendix titled "What You Should Know About Endangered Species" offers facts about threatened and endangered plants and animals in the United States and around the world. The appendix "What You Should Do About Endangered Species" offers ways that young people can help protect fragile populations. With all these features, *Issues That Concern You: Endangered Species* provides an excellent resource for everyone interested in this issue.

ONE

The Earth Is Losing Species at an Alarming Rate

Scott LaFee

> In the following viewpoint journalist Scott LaFee reports that earth is in the process of its sixth "mass-extinction event," or a period when more than half of its living species will become extinct. But unlike the earlier mass extinctions, caused by such events as asteroids hitting earth or geological disasters, this one has been caused almost exclusively by human activity, according to many scientists. Unless humans stop the behaviors that lead to so much habitat loss and climate change, the viewpoint concludes, human beings may be among the species that become extinct before earth recovers. LaFee, a staff writer for the *San Diego Union-Tribune*, writes frequently about scientific issues.

On March 2 [2009], an asteroid discovered just three days earlier narrowly missed the Earth. Dubbed 2009 DD45, it passed within 47,000 miles of the planet—a distance only slightly more than twice the altitude of a geostationary communications satellite. The moon is five times farther away.

It was a relatively small asteroid: 100 to 130 feet in diameter, roughly the size of the comet or asteroid that flattened Russia's Tunguska River region in 1908. If 2009 DD45 had actually collided with Earth, it would not have ended life as we know it. We're doing that ourselves.

Over the past 500 million years, the Earth has endured five mass-extinction events, periods when 50 to more than 90 percent of all known species perished. The last event—the Cretaceous-Tertiary event 65 million years ago, which spelled the end of the dinosaurs—was likely instigated by the impact of an asteroid far larger than 2009 DD45. But other phenomena have been cited as possible causes of mass-extinction events, including massive volcanism and extreme climate change.

Now, most scientists agree, we're in the midst of a sixth mass extinction, this one human-induced. What remains to be seen is just how bad it will be.

"Extinction is a difficult phenomenon to measure because we are still counting and describing the number of living species on Earth," said Mark Wilson, a professor of geology at the College of Wooster in Ohio. "We may be losing tens of thousands of species every year which we haven't even met yet."

But there is a sense among researchers that the current mass extinction, known as the Holocene event, will be very bad indeed. In the past, the Earth invariably rebounded, different but alive, eventually refilling with new and more diverse creatures and plants. Life moved on.

Odds are, humans will, too. At this point, scientists tend to think humanity will persist in some form or fashion. As a species, we are remarkably adaptable and resourceful.

The planet, not so much. Phenomena like global climate change and habitat destruction, both powerfully propelled by modern human activities, have fundamentally changed the rules. A University of Leeds study says current emission trends may raise global temperatures by the end of the century to levels not seen in 30 million years. Humans already use about half of all available land on Earth.

"There's this idea of resilience," said Rebecca Lewison, an assistant professor of biology at San Diego State University. "How far can ecosystems be pushed before they permanently collapse? How much ecological havoc can we effect before there can be no rebound? We don't really know what the boundaries are."

The Growing Rate of Extinctions

Extinction is a part of life, with new species inevitably replacing those less able to adapt or compete. Evolution means that more than 90 percent of all species of animal and plant that have ever lived on Earth are now extinct.

But how long should a species persist? Based on the fossil record, the average lifetime of an invertebrate species, from origination to extinction, is estimated at 5 million to 10 million years. Mammal species come and go much more quickly, usually within 1 million to 2 million years.

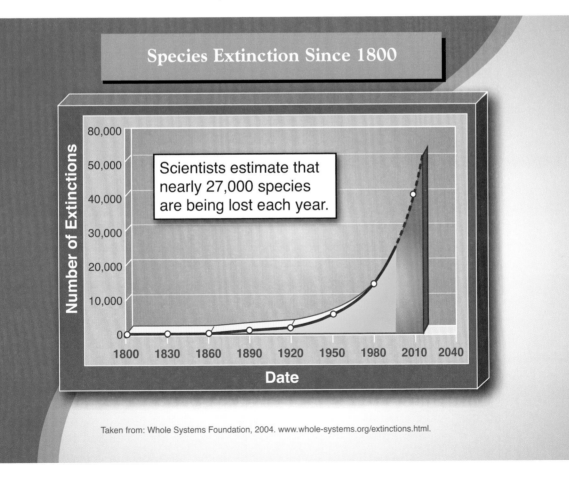

Taken from: Whole Systems Foundation, 2004. www.whole-systems.org/extinctions.html.

Scientists say the "normal background extinction rate" is one species per million per year, with maybe 10 to 25 species disappearing in a year. The current extinction rate is projected at 100 to 1,000 times higher than the normal background rate. "It's unprecedented," said Lewison.

The United Nations Convention on Biological Diversity estimates three species become extinct each hour. That's 72 every day; 26,280 each year.

Exact numbers are debatable, but the point is not: Much of the planet's biota [flora and fauna] is imperiled. The International Union for Conservation of Nature (IUCN), which maintains a highly regarded "Red List" of endangered and threatened species, estimates more than 16,300 species of animal and plant are on the verge of extinction; more than 41,000 are threatened.

The group says one-eighth of all birds, one-third of all amphibians and half of the world's turtles are in jeopardy. Seventy percent of the world's plants are considered at risk.

Blame people, says conservation biologist Michael Soule, who asserts modern extinctions are almost entirely the result of human activity—everything from habitat destruction and the introduction of non-native species to pollution, overexploitation and disease. For example, the United Nations estimates 32 million acres of forest are lost annually, almost half of that total consisting of forest previously undisturbed by man.

Ocean acidity is rising, the result of seawater absorbing more atmospheric carbon dioxide emitted by industry and automobiles. Increased ocean acidity blocks the ability of corals and hard-shelled marine creatures to form, and hinders the growth and reproduction rates of plankton and fish.

In central Africa, the gorilla population has declined 60 percent in the last quarter-century due to local wars, the bush-meat trade and the Ebola virus.

Remnants and Recovery

The ramifications of lost biodiversity are almost impossible to overstate. Recent studies have shown that grassland ecosystems

Stanford professor of population studies Paul Ehrlich notes that since 1993, 408 new species of mammals have been discovered.

with fewer plant species generally produce less biomass (living matter) than ecosystems with more species. Less plant biomass means less atmospheric carbon dioxide is absorbed and less oxygen is produced. A global decline in vegetable biomass can change the composition of gasses in the atmosphere. It means fewer plants for herbivores to eat. Entire food chains may be disrupted.

In a recently published paper, Paul Ehrlich, the Bing professor of population studies at Stanford University, and his wife, Anne, a senior research scientist, noted that since 1993, an astounding 408 new species—of mammals alone—have been discovered.

That might seem like news to celebrate, but Ehrlich, famous for his 1968 book *The Population Bomb*, suggests it also reveals how little we know about the planet's biosphere. "Our analysis indicates how much more varied biodiversity is than we thought and how much bigger our conservation problems are if we're going to maintain the life-support services that we need from biodiversity," Ehrlich said.

He compares nature's biodiversity to the engineered redundancy in an airplane. The "rivet hypothesis" holds that you can lose some rivets in a plane's wing and it will continue to fly, said Ehrlich. At some point, however, the loss of just one more rivet becomes catastrophic.

"Even though you don't know the value of each rivet," said Ehrlich, "you know it's nuttier than hell to keep removing them. There is some redundancy (in nature), but we don't know how much. And facing serious climate disruption, humanity is going to need more redundancy in the little rivets, the species and populations that run the world."

But nothing will improve as long as human behavior and activity do not, said Barry Goldstein, a biology professor at the University of Puget Sound in Washington. "The current event will last as long as habitat loss and rapid climate change continue to occur at the present rate."

And if mass extinction goes on long enough—events have lasted from hundreds of thousands to millions of years—what's left may consist only of "weedy survivors," said Peter Ward, a paleontologist at the University of Washington. These are animals supremely adaptable and opportunistic, such as flies, rats, crows, coyotes and intestinal parasites.

These "recovery fauna" might be the dominant organisms on Earth for a very long time. In a 2000 paper, UC [University of California] Berkeley environmental scientist James Kirchner and Duke University paleontologist Ann Weil found that the average amount of time it took for the Earth's biodiversity to regain levels prior to a mass extinction event was 10 million years. The length of time didn't vary whether an extinction event was large or small.

That's far beyond any human time scale. Modern humans have only been around for a few hundred thousand years. Ancestral hominids date back only a few million years.

A recovery period of 10 million years, said Kirchner at the time of his study, "is well past the expected life span of the human species, or even of the genus Homo."

TWO

The Oceans' Fish Are in Serious Decline

Katharine Mieszkowski

In the viewpoint that follows, journalist Katharine Mieszkowski describes the rapid decline of the world's supply of fish used by humans for food and argues that the decline is due to overfishing. Researchers have demonstrated the harm caused by overfishing, she notes, and have asked governments to set limits on how many fish can be taken, but the scientists' advice has been largely ignored. Unless people stop buying and eating threatened species, she concludes, the economic, social, and environmental consequences will be serious. Mieszkowski, named one of the top twenty-five Women on the Web in 2001, is a senior writer for Salon.com, where she covers technology, business, and the environment.

When it comes to stopping overfishing in coastal ocean waters, there's a whale of a gap between what nations pledge to do and what happens at sea. That's the grim conclusion of a new study published in *PLoS Biology*, the first global assessment of human management of fisheries—designated areas where fish and aquatic animals are caught—whose coauthors include renowned marine biologists such as the late Ransom A. Myers and Boris Worm of Dalhousie University in Nova Scotia.

Katharine Mieszkowski, "Plundering the Oceans," *Salon*, July 1, 2009. This article first appeared in Salon.com, at www.salon.com. An online version remains in the *Salon* archives. Reprinted with permission.

It's well documented that many of the world's major fisheries are in shocking decline. Some 90 percent of the world's big fish, such as bluefin tuna, blue marlin and Antarctic cod, have almost disappeared from the oceans since the advent of industrial fishing in the 1950s, according to a groundbreaking paper published in *Nature* in 2003 by Myers and Worm. And by 2048 the world's supply of seafood will likely simply run out, Worm and other marine biologists warned in the pages of *Science* in 2006. As of 2008, 80 percent of the world's fish stocks were considered either vulnerable to collapse or already collapsed.

This sorry state of affairs has inspired numerous international efforts, such as the United Nations Code of Conduct for Responsible Fisheries and the Convention on Biological Diversity, in hopes of making more of the world's fisheries sustainable. These initiatives have gained broad acceptance on the world stage, with many countries pledging to adhere to their principles. But where the trawler meets the sea, it's a different story. "Unfortunately, our study shows that there is a marked difference between the endorsement of such initiatives and the actual implementation of corrective measures," observe the authors of the report *Management Effectiveness of the World's Marine Fisheries*.

A Survey Says That Enforcement Is Unreliable

Researchers spent a year approaching almost 14,000 fishery experts, including marine biologists, fishery managers and university professors around the globe, asking them to take an online survey in either English, French, Spanish, German or Portuguese about local fishing practices and policies. Almost 1,200 completed the survey from 243 countries and territories, including representatives from every country that borders the ocean. The survey asked the experts about their respective nations' scientific data about fish populations and ecosystems, and how they translated those scientific findings into regulations and enforcement.

The dismal results: Only 7 percent of coastal states did rigorous scientific assessments to generate fishing policies; a pitiful

In a one-year survey of 14,000 fishery experts, United Nations fishery researchers found that not one country in the world demonstrated consistency in managing its fish populations effectively.

1.4 percent have a participatory and transparent process for turning that science into policy; and fewer than 1 percent had strong mechanisms to insure enforcement with fishing policies. "Perhaps the most striking result of our survey was that not a single country in the world was consistently good with respect to all these management attributes," says Camilo Mora, 34, a research biologist at Dalhousie University, who was one of the coauthors of the study. "So which countries are doing well, and which are not, is a question whose answer depends on the specific attribute you are looking at."

Not surprisingly, rich countries had the best scientific assessment of how fish in their waters were doing, and poor countries had the weakest. But both wealthy and developing countries performed badly when it came to converting that science into policies to limit fishing, if for different reasons. "In poor countries, there was a lot of corruption going on," explains Mora. "In rich countries, there were more political and economic pressures on the policymaking. The end result of that is that in both cases, science is not converted into proper regulation." Rich countries did a better job than poor countries enforcing those regulations; in some poor countries, there was no enforcement at all.

An Overwhelming Demand

But there's a catch. While rich countries may do a better job policing fishing in their own coastal waters, they are globalizing overfishing by sending their industrial fishing fleets to hoover up the catch near poor countries. Thirty-three percent of the poorest countries in the world sell the right to fish in their waters to some of the richest countries in the world, including those in the European Union, the United States, Taiwan, China, Japan and South Korea.

Seafood makes up at least 15 percent of all animal protein consumed by humans, either directly, or indirectly as feed for the aquaculture and livestock industries. Demand for it is expected to rise as the human population increases. Fisheries employ 200 million people around the world, generating $85 billion annually.

But overfishing won't just change what's on the end of homo sapiens' forks, and who makes money to put it there.

"The consequences of overexploiting the world's fisheries are a concern not only for food security and socioeconomic development but for ocean ecosystems," says Worm, who was one of the coauthors of the paper, in a statement. "We now recognize that overfishing can also lead to the erosion of biodiversity and ecosystem productivity."

While Mora calls on governments to become more transparent about how fishing regulations are created to help prevent outside pressures from influencing those regulations, he also says that there's a lot that individuals can do. "The general public needs to become more aware of the consequences of the things that we consume," he says. "I can't see any excuse for a person to eat a bluefin tuna or a shark. These species are going extinct, and the reason for that is because of the demand for them."

THREE

American Birds Are at Risk

U.S. North American Bird Conservation Initiative

> The following viewpoint originally appeared as part of the *State of the Birds, United States of America 2009* report, a comprehensive analysis of the health of American bird populations conducted by the U.S. North American Bird Conservation Initiative, a group of governmental and private conservation agencies and organizations. According to the authors, thriving bird populations indicate a thriving nation that has taken proper care of its air and water, but declining populations, as are seen in many parts of the United States, indicate damaged and dwindling habitats. Although wetland birds have done well over the past forty years, the viewpoint concludes, more cooperation is needed between government and private groups to protect other birds and the natural landscapes where they live.

The United States is blessed with diverse landscapes, a wealth of natural resources, and spectacular wildlife, including more than 800 bird species. Birds are a national treasure and a heritage we share with people around the world, as billions of migratory birds follow the seasons across oceans and continents. Our passion for nature is evident: Wildlife

U.S. North American Bird Conservation Initiative, *State of the Birds* 2009, March 19, 2009. www.stateofthebirds.org. Reproduced by permission.

watching generates $122 billion in economic output annually, and one in every four American adults is a bird watcher.

In the past 200 years, however, the U.S. human population has skyrocketed from about 8 million to 300 million. As we have harvested energy and food, grown industries, and built cities, we have often failed to consider the consequences to nature. During our history, we have lost a part of our natural heritage—and degraded and depleted the resources upon which our quality of life depends. We have lost more than half of our nation's original wetlands, 98% of our tallgrass prairie, and virtually all virgin forests east of the Rockies. Since the birth of our nation, four American bird species have gone extinct, including the Passenger Pigeon, once the world's most abundant bird. At least 10 more species are possibly extinct.

Tragic Environmental Indicators

Birds are bellwethers of our natural and cultural health as a nation—they are indicators of the integrity of the environments that provide us with clean air and water, fertile soils, abundant wildlife, and the natural resources on which our economic development depends. In the past 40 years, major public, private, and government initiatives have made strides for conservation. Has it been enough? How are birds faring?

In an unprecedented partnership, government wildlife agencies and conservation groups have come together to produce this first comprehensive analysis of the state of our nation's birds. The results are sobering: bird populations in many habitats are declining—a warning signal of the failing health of our ecosystems. Where we have been negligent too long, such as in Hawaii, we are on the verge of losing entire suites of unique and beautiful birds and native plant communities.

At the same time, we see heartening evidence that birds can respond quickly and positively to conservation action. Many waterfowl species have undergone significant increases in the past 40 years, a testament to coordinated conservation efforts in wetlands. Through focused conservation efforts, we have brought

Federal wildlife officials plan to spend 14 million dollars to save the Hawaiian black crow, the alala, from extinction.

magnificent Peregrine Falcons and Bald Eagles back from the brink of extinction.

We ask you to join us in continuing to reverse the damage to our nation's habitats and protect our remaining natural landscapes—the foundation upon which our precious resources, our wildlife, and the lives of our children depend. Cooperative conservation efforts among the government, conservation organizations, and ordinary citizens—private landowners, hunters, and bird watchers—really are making a difference.

It is imperative that we redouble our efforts now, before habitat loss and degradation become even more widespread, intractable, and expensive to solve. Together, we can ensure that future generations will look back at this first *State of the Birds* report with disbelief that their common birds could ever have been so troubled.

The State of Our Nation's Birds

The United States is home to a tremendous diversity of native birds, with more than 800 species inhabiting terrestrial, coastal, and ocean habitats, including Hawaii. Among these species, 67 are federally listed as endangered or threatened. An additional 184 are species of conservation concern because of their small distribution, high threats, or declining populations. . . .

Every U.S. habitat harbors birds in need of conservation. Hawaiian birds and ocean birds appear most at risk, with populations in danger of collapse if immediate conservation measures are not implemented. Bird populations in grassland and aridland habitats show the most rapid declines over the past 40 years. Birds that depend on forests are also declining.

In contrast, wetland species, wintering coastal birds, and hunted waterfowl show increasing populations during the past 40 years, reflecting a strong focus during this period on wetlands conservation and management.

More than one-third of all U.S. listed bird species occur in Hawaii and 71 bird species have gone extinct since humans colonized the islands in about 300 A.D. At least 10 more birds have not been seen in as long as 40 years and may be extinct. Proven conservation measures are urgently needed to avert this global tragedy, including increasing investment in protecting remaining forests, eliminating exotic predators, and captive breeding.

At least 39% of the U.S. birds restricted to ocean habitats are declining. These birds face threats from pollution, over-fishing, and warming sea temperatures caused by climate change, as well as threats at island and coastal nesting sites.

Declining seabirds may be our most visible indication of an ocean ecosystem under stress.

Although some coastal birds are increasing, shorebirds that rely on coastal habitats for breeding and refueling on migration are besieged by human disturbance and dwindling food supplies. Sea level rise caused by accelerating climate change will inundate shoreline habitats. Half of all coastally migrating shorebirds have declined; for example, Red Knots have declined by an alarming 82%. Because of their relatively small and highly threatened global populations, shorebirds are of high conservation concern.

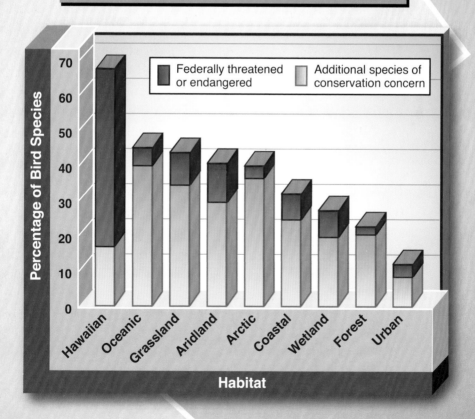

Most Bird Habitats in the United States Need Conserving

Taken from: *State of the Birds 2009*, www.stateofthebirds.org/overview.

The upward trend for wetland birds in the U.S. is a testament to the amazing resilience of bird populations where the health of their habitat is sustained or restored. The overwhelming success of waterfowl management, coordinated continentally among Canada, the United States, and Mexico, can serve as a model for conservation in other habitats.

Dramatic declines in grassland and aridland birds signal alarming degradation of these often neglected habitats. Incentives for wildlife-compatible agricultural practices in grasslands and increased protection of fragile desert, sagebrush, and chaparral ecosystems are urgently needed to reverse these declines.

Although forest birds have fared better overall than birds in other habitats, many species have suffered steep declines and remain threatened by unplanned and sprawling urban development, unsustainable logging, increased severity of wildfires, and a barrage of exotic forest pests and disease, which will likely be exacerbated by climate change.

Conservation Efforts Must Come from All Sides

The will of our nation to prevent extinction and reverse environmental degradation is exemplified by the remarkable recovery of the Bald Eagle, Peregrine Falcon, and other bird populations after the banning of harmful pesticides such as DDT. Although targeted conservation programs for listed species remain necessary, proactive measures involving voluntary partnerships between local, state, tribal, and federal government, nongovernmental organizations, and private citizens are needed to maintain the integrity of U.S. habitats and to keep our common birds common.

Over the last two decades, unprecedented private-public partnerships, called Joint Ventures, have been highly effective at leveraging scarce funds to conserve millions of acres of wetlands and other wildlife habitat. Also, bird conservation initiatives such as Partners in Flight, the U.S. Shorebird Conservation Plan, and the North American Waterbird Conservation Plan have raised awareness and inspired conservation action at continental and regional scales. These vital activities, along with the implementation of Wildlife Action Plans in all 50 states, are coordinated under the North American Bird Conservation Initiative.

FOUR

The Bald Eagle Is No Longer at Risk

National Audubon Society

> The following viewpoint, originally a press release from the National Audubon Society, celebrates the success of conservation efforts begun in the 1960s to protect the bald eagle, the national bird of the United States of America. The rescue of the bald eagle, the viewpoint argues, demonstrates that giving endangered and threatened species federal protection works. The efforts of federal agencies, including the U.S. Fish and Wildlife Service and the Environmental Protection Agency, made it possible to relocate bald eagles and safeguard them from hazardous pesticides, according to the authors. It will be important in the future, the authors conclude, to strengthen and enforce the Endangered Species Act and other laws that protect species. The National Audubon Society, founded in 1905, is one of the oldest and largest conservation organizations in the world.

Citizen science is confirming the wisdom of an historic action that federal officials plan to formalize within days—removing the resurgent bald eagle from the protection of the Endangered Species Act. [The bald eagle was delisted from its federal threatened status on June 28, 2007.] The National

National Audobon Society, "Bald Eagle Back from the Brink," June 26, 2007. www.audubon.org. Reproduced by permission.

Audubon Society says actual bald eagle sightings in the century-old Christmas Bird Count reveal that the national bird's populations are continuing a steady climb in the lower 48 states, underscoring its amazing return from the brink.

"The rescue of the bald eagle from the brink of extinction ranks among the greatest victories of American conservation," said John Flicker, President of the National Audubon Society. "Like no other species, the bald eagle showed us all that environmental stewardship has priceless rewards. In every state, parents and grandparents can still point to the sky and share a moment of wonder as a bald eagle soars overhead."

The success is evident in the Audubon counts. Over a 40-year period from 1967 to 2006, bald eagle sightings have gone up nine-fold and increased an average of six percent per year every year. The top five states with the most dramatic increases

The rescue of the American bald eagle from extinction demonstrates that the Endangered Species Act is working for threatened species.

were Ohio, Pennsylvania, West Virginia, Vermont and Michigan, which all had at least a 13-fold increase over 40 years.

"Audubon's bird count data confirms that the bald eagle has recovered across America," says Greg Butcher, Audubon's Director of Bird Conservation. "Audubon's count shows that Americans are seeing the bald eagle's recovery beyond the numbers and the technical reports. They're seeing it in their skies."

A symbol of national strength and unity, the bald eagle has also become a parable for nature's unshakable ties to humans—for better or worse. Estimated to have numbered 100,000 in precolonial times, shooting, cutting of forests, and finally pesticides, took a toll on the bird, bringing it to the brink of extinction by the early 1960's. Strong federal and state protection and the banning of [the pesticide] DDT brought the bird back from the brink. Very soon, the bald eagle is expected to soar off of the endangered and threatened list, assuming a new symbolic role as America's best conservation success.

"This is a victory worth celebrating—and protecting," adds Flicker. "How fitting that our nation's symbol soars off the Endangered Species list as we prepare to celebrate America's independence."

Resurgence of a National Icon

Bald eagle populations declined dramatically in the last century, attributed mostly to the accumulation of the pesticide DDT in fish, a staple of the eagle's diet. The pesticides gradually poisoned females, causing them to produce thinly-shelled eggs that broke easily, preventing the embryos from growing. Years of hunting, accidental poisoning and habitat loss took an additional toll.

In 1960, Audubon took the lead in studying the eagle's declines through its Continental Bald Eagle Project. The project revealed that DDT was in large part responsible for population declines among several raptor species including the bald eagle.

The U.S. Fish and Wildlife Service (FWS) in 1967 listed the bald eagle as endangered, a designation that gave the bird legal protection from harmful human activities and in 1972, the

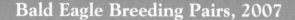

Bald Eagle Breeding Pairs, 2007

Approximately 9,789 breeding pairs of bald eagles exist in the lower forty-eight states.

WA 848
OR 470
MT 325
ND 15
MN 1,312
NH
VT
ME 414
1 12
ID 216
SD 41
WI 1,065
MI 482
NY 110
MA 25
WY 95
IA 200
PA 96
RI 1
NV 3
NE 37
IL 100
IN 68
OH 125
19
WV
VA 485
CT 10
NJ 53
UT 9
CO 42
MO 123
KY 35
DE 39
CA 200
KS 23
NC 60
MD 400
AZ 43
NM 4
OK 49
AR 42
TN 120
SC 208
DC 1
MS 31
AL 77
GA 82
TX 156
LA 284
FL 1,133

Taken from: U.S. Fish & Wildlife Service, April 2007.
www.fws.gov/migratorybirds/CurrentBirdIssues/BaldEagle/baldeaglepopmapfinal.pdf.

U.S. Environmental Protection Agency banned most uses of DDT. Listing the bald eagle afforded greater protection for important habitat, and saw the beginning of intensive monitoring and management of bald eagle populations in the wild as well as introduction of eagles from Alaska, Wisconsin, and other states to areas of the country where they had disappeared.

By the mid-90s, the eagle was well on the road to recovery and the FWS "downlisted" the bald eagle from endangered to threatened in most states under the Endangered Species Act (ESA). Today, the FWS estimates there are over 7,000 nesting pairs of bald eagles in the continental United States.

The eagle's success is not a trend shared by bird populations nationwide. A recent analysis on common birds in decline conducted by Audubon found the average population of the common birds in steepest decline had fallen by 68 percent; and some individual species nose-dived as much as 80 percent. All 20 birds on the national *Common Birds in Decline* list lost at least half their populations in just four decades.

Ongoing Controversy

After delisting, the bald eagle will remain under federal protection largely through the Bald and Golden Eagle Protection Act of 1940, as well as a patchwork of state laws. There is some controversy surrounding proposed [President George W.] Bush administration regulations regarding how easily permits would be issued allowing developers and other parties to disrupt bald eagle nests. Audubon will be advocating tighter regulations that would limit the ease with which these permits may be granted. In some areas, special protection may also be needed to protect distinct eagle populations.

In addition, the law that was instrumental in recovering the bald eagle, the Endangered Species Act, remains a target of pro-development interests and their allies in the Bush administration. The administration is expected to introduce regulations soon that would weaken the ESA's ability to protect species and their habitat. The effort follows years of attacks on the ESA prior to the change in Congressional leadership in 2007.

FIVE

The Polar Bear Should Have Federal Protection as a Threatened Species

Brendan P. Kelly

> In the following viewpoint marine biologist Brendan P. Kelly draws on his own thirty years of research on the marine mammals in and near the Arctic Ocean to argue that sea ice, an essential component of the habitat of polar bears and other animals, is rapidly disappearing. The loss of sea ice, he continues, threatens polar bears' survival by making it more difficult for them to breed cubs and to find food. Because the sea ice is melting so quickly, he concludes, the polar bear should be listed as a threatened species so that it may have the protection of the federal government under the Endangered Species Act. Kelly is the vice provost for research at the University of Alaska Southeast.

For over thirty years, I have studied the marine mammals that populate the Gulf of Alaska as well as the Bering, Chukchi, and Beaufort seas. During those three decades, I have witnessed dramatic changes in the sea ice that provides essential habitat to 7 species of seals, walruses, and polar bears. Eleven of the 12

Brendan P. Kelly, "Testimony Submitted to Senate Committee on Environment and Public Works," U.S. Senate Committee on Environmental and Public Works, January 30, 2008. http://epw.senate.gov.

warmest years since 1850 were recorded between 1994 and 2006, and one result has been that the seasonal duration and extent of the ice decreased substantially. . . . The Intergovernmental Panel on Climate Change, the American Geophysical Union, and the vast majority of sea ice physicists predict that there will be no summer sea ice in the Arctic Ocean before the current century is over, perhaps within the next 30 years.

The loss of over 8,000,000 km² of summer sea ice will endanger many species of plants and animals adapted to that once extensive habitat. Polar bears especially will be negatively impacted as they are adapted to a narrow niche, namely hunting seals from the sea ice.

Polar Bears' Specialized Diet Depends on Sea Ice

The narrow niche occupied by polar bears can be contrasted to that of brown bears who occupy a greater range of habitats and whose diet is much broader. Genetic data indicate that polar bears began to separate from a brown bear population (probably in southern Alaska) 150,000 to 250,000 years ago. Molecular biology does not tell us when that new line of bears began to specialize in hunting Arctic seals, but the oldest fossils showing the specialized meat-eating teeth that distinguish today's polar bears from brown bears are as recent as 20,000 years old.

Specialization to preying on ice-inhabiting seals was not without its costs, and the polar bear's feeding success is strongly related to ice conditions; when stable ice is over productive shelf waters, polar bears can feed throughout the year on their primary prey, ringed seals. When the ice is absent, however, the bears lack a platform from which to capture surfacing seals.

Today, an estimated 20,000 to 25,000 polar bears live in 19 apparently discrete populations distributed around the circumpolar Arctic. Their overall distribution largely matches that of ringed seals, which inhabit all seasonally ice-covered seas in the Northern Hemisphere, an area extending in winter to approximately 15,000,000 km². The broad distribution of their seal prey is reflected in the home ranges of polar bears which—averaging

Vanishing Sea Ice and Snow

Rapid warming in the Arctic has led to less sea ice and snow cover—and less area for polar bears to make their dens.

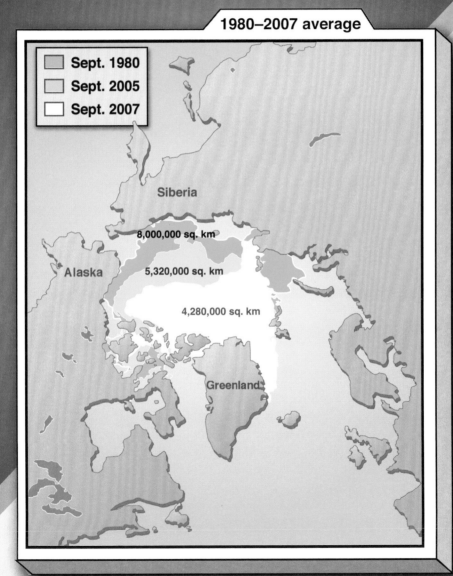

1980–2007 average

Sept. 1980
Sept. 2005
Sept. 2007

Siberia

8,000,000 sq. km

5,320,000 sq. km

Alaska

4,280,000 sq. km

Greenland

Taken from: National Snow and Ice Data Center, 2008.

over 125,000 km^2—are 200 times larger than the averages for brown bears. Most polar bear populations expand and contract their range seasonally with the distribution of sea ice, and they spend most of [the] year on the ice. Most populations, however, retain their ancestral tie to the terrestrial environment for denning, although denning on the sea ice is common among the bears of the Beaufort and Chukchi seas. Dens on land and on ice are excavated in snow drifts, the stability and predictability of which are essential to cub survival.

The rapid rates of warming in the Arctic observed in recent decades and projected for at least the next century are dramatically reducing the snow and ice covers that provide denning and foraging habitat for polar bears. These changes to their environment will exert new, strong selection pressures on polar bears. Adaptive traits reflect selection by past environments, and the time needed to adapt to new environments depends on genetic diversity in populations, the intensity of selection, and the pace of change. Genetic diversity among polar bears is evident in the 19 putative populations, suggesting some scope for adaptation within the species as a whole even if some populations will be at greater risk than others. On the other hand, the nature of the environmental change affecting critical features of polar bears' breeding and foraging habitats, and the rapid pace of change relative to the bears' long generation time (about 15 years) do not favor successful adaptation.

The most obvious change to breeding habitats is the reduction in the snow cover on which successful denning depends. Female polar bears hibernate for four to five months per year in snow dens in which they give birth to cubs, typically twins, each weighing just over 1 lb. The small cubs depend on snow cover to insulate them from the cold.

Threats to Polar Bears' Way of Life

Changes in the foraging habitat that will entail new selection pressures include seasonal mismatches between the energetic demands of reproduction and prey availability; changes in prey

The rapid increase in Arctic temperatures has significantly reduced the ice cover on which polar bears depend for survival.

abundance; changes in access to prey; and changes in community structure.

Emergence of female and young polar bears from dens in the spring coincides with the ringed seal's birthing season, and the newly emerged bears depend on catching and consuming young seals to recover from months of fasting. The match in timing between bear emergence and the availability of young seals may be disrupted by changes in timing and duration of snow and ice cover. Such mismatches between reproductive cycles and food availability are increasingly recognized as a means by which a variety of animal populations are impacted by climate change.

Recognized as the most abundant of northern seals, ringed seal populations also are likely to decline as the sea ice habitat changes. Like polar bears, ringed seals depend on snow caves for rearing their young, and increasingly early snow melts have led to high rates of seal mortality due to hypothermia and predation. Walruses and bearded seals also are preyed upon by polar bears, and feeding and reproduction of those animals likewise is tightly coupled to the sea ice environment.

The polar bear's ability to capture seals depends on the presence of ice. In that habitat, bears take advantage of the fact that seals must surface to breathe in limited openings in the ice cover. In the open ocean, however, bears lack a hunting platform, seals are not restricted in where they can surface, and successful predation is exceedingly rare. Only in ice-covered waters are bears regularly successful at hunting seals. When restricted to shorelines, bears feed little if at all, and terrestrial foods generally are of little significance to polar bears.

Seal and other prey populations also will be impacted by fundamental changes in the fate of primary production. For example, in the Bering and Chukchi seas, the reduction in sea ice cover alters the physical oceanography in ways that diminish nutrient flow to bottom-dwelling organisms and increases nutrient recycling closer to the ocean surface. The resultant shift in the composition of the biological community will impact all branches of the food web, including polar bears. The exact composition of future biological communities in the Arctic Ocean is not known, nor is it known how effectively polar bears might exploit those communities.

Polar Bears Face Possible Extinction

The rapid rate at which snow and ice cover is declining will work against successful adaptation by polar bears. Populations are likely to be reduced and extinction could result from mortality outpacing production and/or from hybridization with brown bears.

The U.S. Fish and Wildlife Service has made a careful analysis of the threats and prudently recommended listing polar bears as threatened. They accurately summarized the preponderance of evidence that the loss of sea ice will threaten polar bears. They have used the best available information to project likely changes in population levels. We cannot expect those projections to be precise in terms of actual numbers, but we have every reason to believe that population changes will be large and downward given the magnitude of sea ice loss.

The impacts of small changes in habitat can be difficult to predict, but the impacts of whole-sale loss of critical habitat are more obvious. If a lake shrinks, its fish population likely will be stressed but survival of the population is quite possible. If the lake dries up completely—even if only seasonally—the fish population will not survive. Sea ice is essential habitat to polar bears just as lake water is to fish, and the U. S. Fish and Wildlife Service's proposal to list polar bears as threatened is appropriate and timely.

SIX

The Polar Bear Does Not Need Federal Protection

Kenneth P. Green

In the viewpoint that follows, Kenneth P. Green argues that many people are concerned about the polar bear because it is popular and attractive, not because it is genuinely threatened by extinction. In fact, he contends, polar bears seem to be strong and resilient, but scientists know very little about the health of polar bear populations because the bears' remoteness makes them difficult to study, and no large body of data about their habitat exists. It would be a mistake, he concludes, to extend federal protection for polar bears— protection that would limit important economic activities, including energy exploration and production—based on limited scientific knowledge. Green, an environmental scientist, is a research scholar at the American Enterprise Institute, a private institution dedicated to research and education on issues of government, politics, economics, and social welfare.

Environmentalists have long used charismatic megafauna— large animals that invoke powerful attachments in humans —to raise awareness of and promote policy solutions to perceived environmental threats. Giant pandas, the symbol of

Kenneth P. Green, "Is the Polar Bear Endangered, or Just Conveniently Charismatic?" AEI Outlook Series, May 2008. Reproduced with the permission of the American Enterprise Institute for Public Policy Research, Washington, DC.

the World Wide Fund for Nature [WWF], are a type of charismatic megafauna, as are "whales and other sea mammals, salmon and other inspirational fish, eagles and other flashy raptors." Other charismatic megafauna featured in environmental crusades include gorillas, grizzly bears, wolves, great white sharks, the Arctic lynx, African elephants, bighorn sheep, rhinoceroses, and, of course, penguins, which got a movie of their very own.

Warm and Cuddly Animals Attract Charity

Such campaigns are highly effective. Environmental activist Eric de Place observes that using these types of animals as "poster children" for broader conservation has worked with grizzly bears, wolves, and sea otters. And the money follows the glamour. Studies have shown that our spending preferences skew to the charismatic species: as economist Robert Stavins points out, the species we protect are generally "warm and cuddly."

The latest animal to become an environmental pet project is *Ursus maritimus*, the Latin name given to the polar bear. In the age of Knut—the polar bear cub orphaned by its mother and raised by humans in a German zoo—media coverage of polar bears has increased dramatically. And, of course, [former vice president] Al Gore featured the plight of the polar bear in his movie *An Inconvenient Truth*.

Polar bears are cute as cubs and majestic as adults. There are few animals with a higher "awwwwww" factor than a baby polar bear, and pictures of adult polar bears standing on icebergs in the far extremes of the Arctic cause an instinctual upwelling of respect for the powerful animals capable of surviving in an environment that humans can tread only with great preparation, and still at great risk. Virtually everyone wishes to ensure that polar bears are protected from excesses of human action that, as we have seen in the past, can indeed drive animal populations to extinction. . . .

As [astronomer] Carl Sagan observed, "Extraordinary claims require extraordinary evidence." This should be especially true when the stakes are significant and are likely to impose considerable costs or limitations on economic development. Walling off the Arctic and enabling environmental groups to sue greenhouse gas emitters in the name of polar bear protection would certainly impose high costs on future generations for whom environmentalists propose to preserve the polar bear.

So we must ask: is there "extraordinary evidence" that polar bears are threatened by man-made global warming sufficient to justify the remarkable claim of setting aside Arctic development and regulating the energy economy of the world for the sake of the animal? . . .

The Health of Polar Bear Populations

Though they are highly photogenic creatures, polar bears are difficult to study for a variety of reasons. First, polar bears live in remarkably isolated and inhospitable parts of the Arctic. Second, polar bears are not stationary animals: they have a very large "home range"—the largest area that an animal normally visits during its lifetime—that often exceeds two hundred thousand square kilometers. . . . And third, the Arctic is such a hostile environment that one can conduct polar bear surveys only at certain times of year and in areas close to land masses. Survey results, therefore, may or may not be representative of the population as a whole. This makes establishing the health of existing polar bear populations—the very beginning of our inquiry—difficult.

Because they are not able to do a rigorous count of existing polar bears or accurately count the number of polar bear offspring over time, scientists must make population estimates based on limited data. Polar bears are counted by periodic flyovers of suspected polar bear habitat or by capturing and marking a subpopulation of bears, then using the frequency of recapture as a means to estimate the size of a population. Few subpopulations have been surveyed repeatedly, and the surveys that exist were taken over different years, some dating back to the 1980s. Where even these limited data are unavailable, population estimates are created basically from hearsay: local peo-

Because polar bears roam freely in isolated and inhospitable environments, they are not easily accessible to researchers for study.

ple report seeing a certain number of polar bears to researchers, who then estimate what size population would be needed to support such a number of sightings. . . .

Because scientists have limited population data for polar bear populations, and even less data on trends in these populations, claims about endangerment are essentially based on assumptions. The first assumption is that global warming has caused, and will cause, a predictable reduction in sea ice. The second assumption holds that polar bear populations will dwindle because they are dependent on sea ice to hunt for prey. But each of these assumptions is fraught with problems.

As with most everything involving climate change, there is a paucity of good-quality, long-term data available. Prior to 1979, the extent of Arctic sea ice was measured haphazardly and sporadically. Some localized, nonstandardized measurements were taken periodically by ships without advanced positioning equipment and are not considered accurate. Satellite imaging has only allowed measurement from about 1979, coinciding with a period of climate warming, which makes it inherently nonrepresentative of longer time periods. . . .

Polar Bears Are Robust Creatures

At present, polar bear populations are robust and, according to native people, are considerably larger than they were in previous decades. Predictions of polar bear endangerment are based on two sets of computer models: one set predicts how much Arctic sea ice will melt as a result of global warming, and the other predicts how polar bear populations will respond. But computer models of climate are known to be fraught with problems, and the ecological models used to predict polar bear response are equally limited.

Because of extreme limitations in data, it is essentially impossible to decide whether polar bears are endangered and whether their habitat is threatened by man-made global warming or other natural climate cycles. This is acknowledged by the experts themselves—the actual IUCN/SSC [International Union for Conservation of Nature/Species Survival Commission] report is more broad in naming causes and more conservative about estimating their effects.

What we do know about polar bears is that, contrary to media portrayals, they are not fragile "canary in the coal mine" animals [the first to be weakened by hazardous conditions], but are robust creatures that have survived past periods of extensive deglaciation. Polar bear fossils have been dated to over one hundred thousand years, which means that polar bears have already survived an interglacial period when temperatures were considerably warmer than they are at present and when, quite probably, levels of summertime Arctic sea ice were correspondingly low.

In discussions of whether to drill in the Arctic, one of the arguments raised by environmentalists is that this would harm

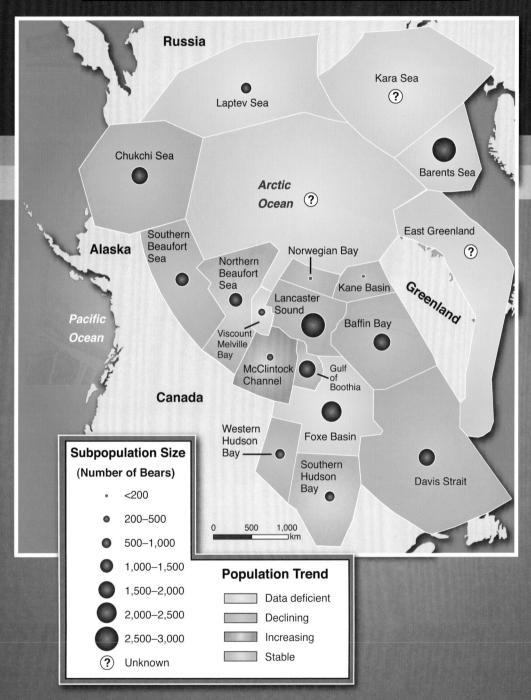

Status of the Arctic Polar Bear, 2009

Subpopulation Size
(Number of Bears)

- ·   <200
- 200–500
- 500–1,000
- 1,000–1,500
- 1,500–2,000
- 2,000–2,500
- 2,500–3,000
- **?**   Unknown

Population Trend

- Data deficient
- Declining
- Increasing
- Stable

Taken from: World Wildlife Federation, 2009. www.panda.org/what_we_do/where_we_work/arctic/area/species/polarbear/population.

the habitats of the many creatures, including polar bears, that make their homes in Alaska. If polar bears are placed on the endangered species list, the legal hurdles to oil and gas drilling will increase. There are two subpopulations of polar bears in Alaska. One of them, the Southern Beaufort Sea population, is shared with Canada, and the other, the Chukchi Sea population, with Russia. Best estimates for these areas show approximately 3,500 polar bears total in these two subpopulations. Last year [2007], Shell Offshore Inc. was about to start drilling in the Beaufort Sea area when a court order halted the activity on the grounds that the federal government did not thoroughly assess the environmental impact before granting permission to drill.

In petitioning against the drilling, environmental groups invoked sea ducks, whales, and, of course, polar bears, as well as the effect that drilling could have on native populations. The U.S. Minerals Management Service estimates that the area holds the potential for 7 billion barrels of recoverable oil and 32 trillion cubic feet of recoverable natural gas. With oil at over $100 a barrel and natural gas at $7.60 per one thousand cubic feet, these are some very expensive polar bears.

Deep-Diving Whales Are Threatened by Navy Sonar

Earthjustice

The following viewpoint reports on the death of a Cuvier's beaked whale, which stranded itself on a beach and died in July 2008 during an exercise in which the U.S. Navy was testing its sonar capabilities. The authors argue that the whale's death may have been caused by the naval exercises and that the navy is not doing all it can to protect marine animals when it uses its mid-range sonar. The navy has denied responsibility for harming animals, the authors conclude, and has defied court orders to take further protective measures. The authors are members of Earthjustice, a large environmental law firm that filed suit in 2007 in an attempt to stop high-intensity, mid-frequency active sonar in anti-submarine exercises in Hawai`i's waters.

A Cuvier's beaked whale stranded and later died on Moloka`i's southeast shore yesterday [July 28, 2008] as the Navy conducted its multi-national Rim of the Pacific (RIMPAC) exercise in Hawai`i's waters, including use of high-intensity, mid-frequency active sonar. Earlier this year, federal district judge David A. Ezra agreed with Ocean Mammal Institute, the Animal Welfare Institute, KAHEA: The Hawaiian-Environmental Alliance, the

Earthjustice, "Whale Killed During Navy Sonar Exercises," July 29, 2008. www.earthjustice.org. Reproduced by permission.

Center for Biological Diversity, and the Surfrider Foundation's Kaua`i Chapter, represented by Earthjustice, that the Navy had been violating federal environmental laws and that the Navy's "protective measures" for its undersea warfare exercises using sonar do not adequately protect whales. Judge Ezra ordered the Navy to add additional measures to reduce the potential to injure or kill marine mammals. The court's injunction did not specifically apply to the RIMPAC exercises, however.

The State Coastal Zone Management Program, in addition to requiring these court-ordered protective measures, went a step further and banned mid-frequency sonar noise over 145 dB [decibels] in the state's coastal zone, including during RIMPAC. The Navy refused to comply. "Instead of applying meaningful protections, the Navy insisted on relying on the same measures that courts in Hawai`i and California have found 'woefully inadequate,'" said Marti Townsend of KAHEA. "They have completely ignored the law that authorizes the State to protect Hawai`i's coastal resources with such restrictions."

"The Navy flat-out refused to apply to RIMPAC the protections that both the federal court and the State believed would better protect Hawai`i's marine mammals," said the Ocean Mammal Institute's Marsha Green. "The death of the beaked whale yesterday may well be a result of the Navy's actions."

The Tragic Results of Routine Sonar Exercises

Deep-diving beaked whales have come into the international spotlight as mass strandings around the world have regularly been linked to naval mid-frequency active sonar use. Other deep diving whales, like pygmy sperm whales and pilot whales, have been similarly affected. Notably, naval sonar has been implicated in mass strandings of marine mammals in, among other places, the Bahamas (2000), Greece (1996), Madeira (2000), the Canary Islands (2002), and Spain (2006). In 2004, during RIMPAC exercises, the Navy's sonar was implicated in a mass stranding of up to 200 melon-headed whales in Hanalei Bay, after which a whale calf died.

"Cuvier's beaked whales appear to be particularly susceptible to harm from mid-frequency active sonar," said whale expert Dr. Robin Baird of Cascadia Research. "They may dive deeper and for longer periods than any other species and loud sonar is thought to interrupt their natural diving behavior. The exact mechanism of harm is not known, but whales stranded in association with naval exercises have exhibited gas bubble lesions, somewhat similar to the bends that human divers experience

Shown here is a photo of an adult Cuvier's beaked whale in Hawaiian waters. It is believed that navy sonar confuses the Cuvier and forces it to the surface so rapidly that it dies of decompression.

when they rise too quickly from a long dive." According to the National Marine Fisheries Service's 2007 Biological Opinion evaluating the Navy's sonar exercises, some 81 percent of the whales known to have been involved in sonar-associated stranding events have been Cuvier's beaked whales. Exposure to sonar blasts, which may reach 235 decibels and can be heard for miles underwater, can also cause serious injury or death caused by trauma to acoustic organs, temporary and permanent hearing loss, displacement from preferred habitat, and disruption of feeding, breeding, nursing, communication, sensing and other behaviors essential to survival.

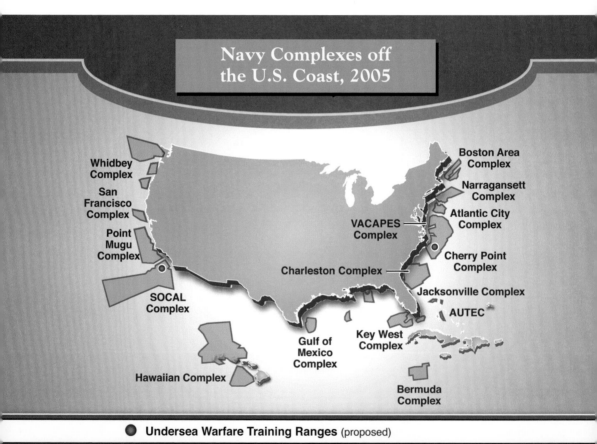

Navy Complexes off the U.S. Coast, 2005

Whidbey Complex

San Francisco Complex

Point Mugu Complex

SOCAL Complex

Hawaiian Complex

Gulf of Mexico Complex

Charleston Complex

VACAPES Complex

Key West Complex

Boston Area Complex

Narragansett Complex

Atlantic City Complex

Cherry Point Complex

Jacksonville Complex

AUTEC

Bermuda Complex

● **Undersea Warfare Training Ranges** (proposed)

Taken from: Michael Jasny, *Sounding the Depths II: The Rising Toll of Sonar, Shipping, and Industrial Ocean Noise on Marine Life*, Natural Resources Defense Council, 2005./Global Security.org and U.S. Department of the Navy. www.nrdc.org/wildlife/marine/sound/sound.pdf.

Following each of two undersea warfare exercises using mid-frequency sonar in Hawai`i's waters in April 2007, dead pygmy sperm whales washed up on Maui county beaches, one carrying a full-term fetus. In February 2008, a female northern right whale dolphin washed up on a Southern California beach as the Navy was completing its sonar exercises nearby. A dissection of the dolphin's head revealed blood and other fluid in its ears and ear canals. The same symptoms were found in deep-diving whales that washed ashore in the Canary Islands and the Bahamas after military sonar exercises.

The Navy routinely denies responsibility for such incidents. Earthjustice attorney Paul Achitoff, who has been litigating the case before Judge Ezra, said, "The Navy's refusal to acknowledge the role it has been playing in causing the deaths of marine mammals around the world, its refusal to follow the findings of every court that has considered these issues, and its refusal to comply with the restrictions lawfully required by Hawai`i's Coastal Zone Management Program, are tragic."

EIGHT

The Navy's First Priority Is National Security

U.S. Department of the Navy

The viewpoint that follows is taken from the U.S. Navy's Web site Ocean Stewardship, which describes the ways in which the navy works to understand and protect marine mammals. Many sources of loud noises are in the ocean, the authors argue, and much is still not known about how whales and other mammals respond to sounds, whether natural or human-caused. Further, they contend, whale strandings occur for many reasons, and most have nothing to do with sonar. But the navy's first responsibility, they conclude, is to defend its sailors and the nation, and sonar is an important part of the navy's defense against enemy submarines.

The ocean is inherently a noisy environment. Seismic disturbances, snapping shrimp and sounds from other ocean dwellers, rain, lightning strikes, and of course manmade sounds such as offshore drilling, seismic surveys, commercial shipping and other ship sounds, fishing boats, recreational boating, and sonar use contribute to the background sound in today's oceans. . . .

The Navy is concerned about the potential effects of active sonar on marine mammals and funds research annually to better understand how marine mammals hear and how they may be af-

Ocean Stewardship, "Understanding Sonar," 2009. www.navy.mil/oceans. Reproduced by permission.

fected by manmade sound. At the same time, the Navy's Title 10 responsibilities under the U.S. Code require us to be prepared for combat at sea to defend the United States, and these responsibilities cannot be met without active sonar and the real-life training required to use it. Based on the technology available today, active sonar is the only effective means for the men and women aboard ship to defend against hostile submarine threats. The Navy will continue to fund research and use mitigation measures to minimize the potential effects of sonar on marine mammals, but cannot put the lives of its Sailors at risk or fail to remain prepared to defend our nation by eliminating active sonar use.

Marine Mammal Protection

For the U.S. Navy, the safety of Sailors and Marines is top priority when carrying out our national security mission. A critical part of this mission is defending Navy ships from the current and future submarine threat. The best way to counter this threat is training with active sonar at sea under simulated combat conditions to detect these submarines before they strike. At the same time, the Navy goes to great lengths to protect marine mammals and the environment during training exercises.

The Navy has implemented an At Sea Policy to guide compliance with environmental requirements in the conduct of naval exercises or training at sea. The policy states that the Navy shall comply with applicable statutes, regulations and executive orders and will strive to protect the environment, prevent pollution, and protect natural, historic, and cultural resources.

Navy policy requires that major fleet exercises be reviewed for environmental compliance and for potential effect on marine mammals and other marine life. Guidance and protective measures, which may be geared to a specific geographic area and date of an exercise, are developed and transmitted to fleet operators as an integral part of fleet exercise planning. Protective measures may include planning to conduct exercises in areas not known to have concentrations of marine mammals; posting

Sounds in the Ocean

The U.S. Navy's mid-frequency active sonar system can transmit sound at approximately 235 decibels, but the loudness diminishes rapidly over the first kilometer of distance from the source. It is unlikely that any animal would experience levels greater than 180 decibels from this system.

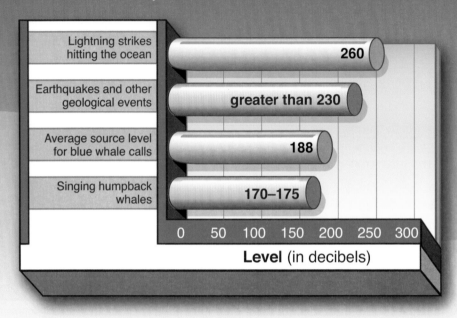

Taken from: U.S. Department of the Navy, "Sonar Allows for Real-Time Training Scenarios and Minimizes Impacts on Marine Animals," *Currents*, Spring 2008, p. 12.

highly trained lookouts; listening for marine mammals with passive hydrophones; creating buffer zones within which operations will be altered or delayed if marine mammals are present; ceasing sonar operations if marine mammals are detected within 200 yards of an active sonar dome, and conducting aerial searches for marine mammals in the area before, during and after sonar operations.

The Navy has developed and implemented procedures throughout the fleet which are designed to help individual ship commanders maintain readiness and protect the environment during routine training and exercises by identifying and employing appropriate protective measures for sensitive marine resources. These measures provide environmental situational awareness as well as specific operating procedures based on place, date and type of training event. The measures emphasize the use of trained lookouts and visual survey capabilities. Therefore, training is planned for daylight hours when possible. For exercises conducted at night, ships rely heavily on passive acoustic monitoring, radar, and/or night vision equipment to survey for protected species and coral reefs.

Stranding Events

According to the National Marine Fisheries Service (NOAA Fisheries), strandings occur when marine mammals or sea turtles swim or float into shore and become beached or stuck in shallow water. Strandings have occurred for hundreds of years and in many parts of the world. According to NOAA Fisheries,

Confused by U.S. Navy sonar, melon-headed whales venture too close to Hawaii's shore. The navy is working to minimize the impact of sonar on marine life, while also ensuring the nation's security.

in 1999 alone, more than 3,000 marine mammals stranded on U.S. shores. In the five years from 1994 through 1998, 19,130 strandings were reported, an average of 3,826 per year.

In most cases, the cause of strandings is unknown, but some identified causes include disease, parasite infestation, harmful algal blooms, injuries from ship strikes or fishery entanglements, exposure to pollution, trauma, and starvation. Strandings also occur after unusual weather or oceanographic events.

Sonar has been linked with only a very small fraction of marine mammal strandings worldwide. One incident, in which several whales stranded in the Bahamas in March of 2000 following a chokepoint exercise, was a confluence of several factors acting together including numbers of sonars, unusual bathymetry, limited egress routes, and specific species of marine mammal. As a result of this incident, the Navy avoids training in coastal areas with bathymetry similar to the Bahamas when possible, and also avoids other known beaked whale concentration areas.

The Navy and NOAA Fisheries learned from the Bahamas stranding that certain marine mammals, particularly beaked whales, may be sensitive to mid-frequency sonar. The Navy is concerned about the potential for sonar to negatively affect marine mammals, and is working with ocean agencies, academic institutions and independent researchers around the world to better understand what combinations of ocean conditions, geography, and sonar use may lead to marine mammal disturbances.

Historical records show that marine mammal strandings have taken place for centuries, well before the advent of sonar. Nonetheless, the Navy remains dedicated to improving the collective understanding of the effects of sonar on marine mammals and to minimizing adverse effects of sonar consistent with our responsibility to defend the nation and ensure the safety of our Sailors, Airmen and Marines. For this purpose, the Navy funds scientific research and implements protective measures as needed to minimize the potential for effects on marine mammals.

NINE

The Endangered Species Act Has Helped Species Recover

Krishna Gifford and Deborah Crouse

> In the following viewpoint Krishna Gifford and Deborah
> Crouse look back on the effects of the Endangered Species
> Act (ESA) in the first thirty-five years since it became law
> in 1973. While political leaders and their attitudes toward
> conservation have changed several times in those years,
> they point out, federal and state agencies have worked
> steadily to safeguard species and their habitats. The act
> has been so successful in protecting endangered and threat-
> ened species, they argue, that fewer than 1 percent of the
> species listed under the law have become extinct. Gifford
> and Crouse are fish and wildlife biologists with the U.S.
> Fish and Wildlife Service's Endangered Species Recovery
> Program.

A lot can happen in three and a half decades. For the U.S. Fish and Wildlife Service, the many changes, challenges, and accomplishments in the conservation of our nation's imper- iled trust resources over the past 35 years have been influenced by a variety of social and natural events.

In terms of our top leadership alone, we have seen 7 Presi- dents (including 5 changes in political parties), 11 Secretaries of

Krishna Gifford and Deborah Crouse, "Thirty-Five Years of the Endangered Species Act," *Endangered Species Bulletin*, Spring 2009.

the Interior, and 8 Service Directors. It is fair to say that their natural resource management philosophies have varied significantly.

We have also witnessed many natural disasters significantly affecting the environment, including catastrophic oil spills (1976 *Argo Merchant*, Buzzards Bay, MA; 1989 *Exxon Valdez*, Prince William Sound, AK; 1990 *Mega Borg*, Galveston, TX; 2000 *Westchester* south of New Orleans, LA; and, in 2005, oil and gas spills from facilities damaged by Hurricane Katrina); major hurricanes (Andrew (1992), Floyd (1999), Katrina (2005), and Ike (2008); major forest fires (summers of 2000, 2002, 2004, and 2007); and drought (1988, 2002, and 2007).

At the same time, each generation is becoming more technologically connected to each other, but less naturally connected to the fish, wildlife, plants, and habitats that the Service works to conserve for the benefit of the American people. With the rise of MTV [music television], video games, the internet, and cell phones, we have seen our children steadily spending less time outdoors.

Significant Achievements

Still, the past 35 years have also brought significant conservation achievements:

- In 2003, the National Wildlife Refuge System celebrated its centennial. There are 548 National Wildlife Refuges (NWRs) and 37 Wetland Management Districts covering more than 96 million acres (39 million hectares). Thirty-nine of these units were established in the last 10 years alone. Fifty-nine NWRs were established specifically for the benefit of imperiled (listed, candidate, species at risk, and other rare) species. Many other units of the National Wildlife Refuge System contribute to conservation of listed species through habitat management.
- There are 65 Fish and Wildlife Conservation Offices, 70 National Fish Hatcheries, 9 Fish Health Centers, and 7 Fish Technology Centers. Most, if not all, of these offices and facilities contribute to the management of listed

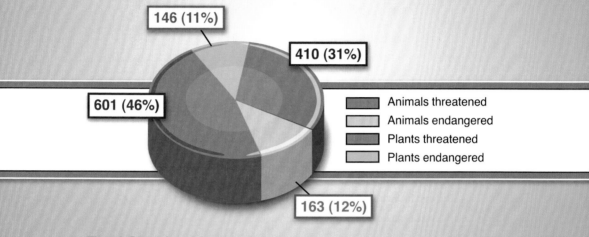

Endangered and Threatened Species in the United States, 2009

The 1,320 species on the federal list of threatened and endangered wildlife and plants are eligible for protection under the Endangered Species Act.

146 (11%)

410 (31%)

601 (46%)

163 (12%)

- Animals threatened
- Animals endangered
- Plants threatened
- Plants endangered

Total Species Listed: 1,320

Taken from: U.S. Fish and Wildlife Service, September 14, 2009. http://ecos.fws.gov/tess_public/TESSBoxscore.

species through propagation, stocking, research, habitat restoration, and other recovery efforts.

- The National Park System (NPS) encompasses 391 areas (parks, monuments, battlefields, military parks, historical parks, historical sites, lakeshores, seashores, recreation areas, and scenic rivers and trails) covering more than 84 million acres (34 million ha [hectares]). Approximately 136 of these areas were established or authorized in the past 35 years. Currently, 465 imperiled species occur on NPS lands, and the National Park Service is an important partner in species conservation and recovery.
- All 50 states and 6 U.S. territories have signed and are implementing State Wildlife Action Plans that strive to keep

wildlife from becoming endangered. All 50 States have also signed cooperative agreements with the Service specifically to conserve endangered and threatened species.

- Finally, the Endangered Species Act (ESA) was signed into law on December 28, 1973. On December 28, 2008, we marked its 35th anniversary. Service staff in 86 Ecological Services or Fish and Wildlife Field Offices, 8 Regional Offices, and the Washington Office, in cooperation with many public and private sector partners, currently administer and implement provisions of the ESA.

When President Richard Nixon signed the ESA, he said, "I congratulate the 93rd Congress for taking this important step toward protecting a heritage which we hold in trust for countless future generations of our fellow citizens." The Fish and Wildlife Service, along with the National Marine Fisheries Service (NMFS) for most marine species, is charged with administering the ESA. To date, with more than 1,300 listed species, only 9 (<1%) have been delisted due to extinction.

The ESA's Methods Are Working

Some of our ESA successes include:

Listings. Over many years, habitat loss, excessive take, the effects of invasive species, and other threats have made it necessary to place more than 1,300 U.S. species on the national lists of threatened and endangered wildlife and plants. With the help of our public and private partners, recovery efforts for these species are underway.

Reclassification (downlisting). A total of 21 U.S. species for which the Service has the lead, and an additional 14 foreign or NMFS-lead species, have been reclassified from endangered to the less critical category of threatened. Aquatic and plant species make up the bulk of these downlistings. Some recently reclassified species include the Florida population of the American crocodile (*Crocodylus acutus*), the Gila trout (*Oncorhynchus gilae*), and the Missouri bladderpod (*Lesquerella filiformis*).

Removal from the list (delisting) due to recovery. Thirteen U.S. species for which the Service has lead, and an additional seven foreign or NMFS-lead species, have been delisted due to recovery. Included in these numbers are species representing different taxa (plants, mammals, reptiles, and birds) from around the United States—east to west coast, mountains to swamps, and Alaska to the Commonwealth of the Northern Mariana Islands. The most recently recovered species include the (West) Virginia

Among the species most recently delisted due to recovery is the West Virginia northern flying squirrel. This is attributable, the authors say, to the success of the Endangered Species Act.

northern flying squirrel (*Glaucomys sabrinus fuscus*), certain populations of the bald eagle (*Haliaeetus leucocephalus*), and the Yellowstone Distinct Population Segment of the grizzly bear (*Ursus arctos horribilis*). Other species are on the brink of delisting due to recovery, including the Maguire daisy (*Erigeron maguirei*), brown pelican (*Pelecanus occidentalis*) rangewide, and Hawaiian hawk or 'io (*Buteo solitarius*).

Recovery Plans. Currently, there are 545 final recovery plans and 48 draft plans that cover 1,129 U.S species for which the Service has the lead. An additional 124 U.S. species have recovery plans under development.

Precluding the need to list. The most effective way to save a species is to conserve it before it reaches the brink of extinction. The Service's and our partners' preventive conservation efforts have made it unnecessary to list 41 U.S. species under the ESA. Some of these species include the Warm Springs Zaitzevian riffle beetle (*Zaitzevia thermae*), blue diamond cholla (*Opuntia whipplei multigeniculata*), Umpqua mariposa lily (*Calochortus umpguaensis*), and Pecos pupfish (*Cyprinodon pecosensis*).

TEN

The Endangered Species Act Harms the Oil and Gas Industry

James M. Inhofe

In the following viewpoint James M. Inhofe warns that the Endangered Species Act (ESA) has been, at most, only a partial success. Although many people praise the bill for protecting endangered and threatened species, he argues that they fail to consider the tremendous costs associated with that protection. Specifically, he contends, ESA requirements that the oil and gas industry in Oklahoma avoid drilling in the habitats of the American burying beetle and the Arkansas River shiner have cost those industries millions of dollars, with little gain. Often, he concludes, protection orders issued under the ESA are not based on good science, and they harm the economy. Inhofe has been a Republican senator from Oklahoma since 1994.

T he oil and gas industry represents 10% of our [Oklahoma's] gross state product and employs more than 55,000 Oklahomans. For the past 15 years, Oklahoma's oil and gas producers paid production taxes in excess of $400 million annually. This money funds schools, roads, health care and other services. A healthy oil and gas industry is critical not only to the livelihood of Oklahomans but to the nation's overall energy security. For

James M. Inhofe, "A Perspective on the Endangered Species Act's Impacts on the Oil and Gas Industry," August 23, 2007. http://epw.senate.gov.

example, 10% of the nation's natural gas reserves are in Oklahoma and for the past two years [2006–2007], the industry has produced energy valued in excess of $10 billion.

It is more important than ever to foster the domestic development of oil and gas resources. Today [at a Senate committee hearing in August 2007], we will hear from witnesses about how the Endangered Species Act [ESA] has impacted that production.

Enacted in 1973, the Endangered Species Act remains one of our most celebrated environmental laws despite the fact that it has not reached many of its stated objectives and has cost the country billions in the process. For example, a 2004 Department of Energy report on natural gas stated that critical habitat designations and section 7 consultations under ESA have caused enormous delays to natural gas projects with an estimated cost to the economy of $261 to $979 million over the past 30 years.

In Oklahoma, the ESA protection of the American Burying Beetle has proven a formidable barrier to oil and gas exploration, production and distribution. The American Burying Beetle was listed in 1989 based on museum collector's data. Nearly 20 years later, actual field data show that the populations of the beetle were and are very extensive. According to the Fish and Wildlife Ecological Service, there may be more than 72,000 beetles in Oklahoma alone. This doesn't sound like a species that is "in danger of extinction."

But the lack of robust science in the listing process is not the only issue. The conservation policies have also taken their toll on the energy industry. . . . The long-standing policy for winter oil and gas construction activities in Oklahoma was suddenly changed without notice to the industry, costing millions of dollars. Unfortunately, changing the rules in the middle of the game is the rule rather than the exception when implementing ESA.

Earlier this year, we got a bit of good news. The Service announced it would begin a status review of the American Burying Beetle; something the ESA requires the Service to do every 5 years. The beetle has been waiting for 13 years. I hope the Service will have some answers for us today about what they have learned and when we can expect some decisions.

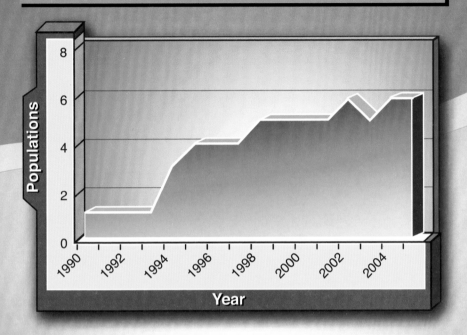

The Rise of Introduced and Captive Burying Beetle Populations in America

Taken from: Center for Biological Diversity, 2005. www.biologicaldiversity.org.

The Costs of Overregulation

The problem goes beyond the oil and gas industry to the consumer, who ultimately pays the price. For example, overregulation drives up natural gas prices for farmers and ranchers, another industry critical to Oklahoma. Natural gas accounts for up to 90% of the total costs of manufacturing fertilizer, an obviously important component of farming. Since 2000, 24 nitrogen fertilizer plants have shut down. Only 6 U.S. plants remain, three of which are in Oklahoma.

And Oklahoma's farmers get hit more than once. They not only face increased natural gas prices but have ESA issues of their own. In an attempt to be good stewards and to avoid the burdensome designation of critical habitat for the Arkansas River Shiner [fish], the Oklahoma Farm Bureau created a voluntary species management plan. . . .

According to the author, protecting the American burying beetle has stifled oil and gas exploration within Oklahoma.

Sadly, the ESA is just one of a host of laws that, although well intended, frustrate domestic energy production in this country. After decades of activist judges and lawsuits by anti-energy special interests, environmental laws are not used to ensure that human actions do not harm the environment but are used to stop human activity altogether. These interests don't believe what all Oklahomans know to be true—that we can develop our energy resources without sacrificing the environment. I am proud that

Oklahoma leads the rest of the country in so many ways when it comes to energy exploration, production, and research, as well as protection of the environment. The Oklahoma Energy Research Board, for example, is a model for many other states.

The fact of the matter is that this engine we call America needs energy to run. If our domestic oil and gas producers are prevented from obtaining that energy, then businesses are hurt and people lose their jobs. Here are just a couple of examples. According to the American Chemistry Council, "one in every 10 chemical-related jobs has vanished in the past five years." The American Forest & Paper Industry "has lost more than 120,000 high paying manufacturing jobs and closed more than 220 plants." In fact, the Pacific Northwest timber industry was essentially shut down 10–15 years ago to protect the Northern Spotted Owl. It is now thought that many of the spotted owl's problems were not from logging but due to competition for food and habitat from other owls.

The obstacles to efficient development of our natural resources are many. Most of them have nothing to do with scarcity of resources, but are created by those in Washington, DC, who say they dislike "relying on foreign oil" but do everything they can to prevent domestic production. When Congress resumes in September [2007], we will have a conference committee to reconcile differences between the Senate and House energy bills. If the goal is to actually improve U.S. energy security, these bills not only fail to meet the mark but they also put in place a new set of roadblocks. I had hoped we could do better.

ELEVEN

Private Property Owners Are the Best Protectors of Wildlife

Terry L. Anderson

In the following viewpoint Terry L. Anderson argues that many hunters and fishers pay too little attention to the private citizens who own land where they can hunt and fish. Without these landowners' efforts to preserve wildlife habitat, he explains, the populations of desirable game animals would be in jeopardy. Citizens who hunt and fish should be careful to vote for candidates who support the rights of private landowners, he concludes. Anderson, a specialist in free market environmentalism, is executive director of the Property and Environment Research Center (PERC), a Montana environmental think tank.

A s sports men and women gear up for the hunting season, they are also being bombarded with information about how they should vote. At the top of the list is gun rights, but they should not forget public access and habitat protection.

On the issue of public access, most hunters and fishers are reveling in the recent court decision declaring the bridges in the state are legitimate stream access points. But before sports people get too excited about fishing everywhere without having to ask permission, they would do well to consider what this

Terry L. Anderson, "Many Private Landowners Nurture Public Wildlife," *Great Falls (MT) Tribune*, October 16, 2008. Reproduced by permission.

means for the landowner's incentive to preserve and improve wildlife habitat.

In both cases the deer, birds, and fish move freely to nearby habitat, public and private. Whether it is trout streams or habitat for big game and "watchable wildlife," private landowners provide a plethora of public benefits, sometimes at substantial costs to themselves.

For example, a study from Montana State University estimates that on private land in Montana big game animals consume forage worth more than $31 million—forage that would otherwise go to feed the landowner's livestock. For this, sports people can thank the private landowner who literally provides a free lunch.

But is it enough to depend on the benevolence of the private landowner? The great conservationist Aldo Leopold thought not. He is known for trying to inculcate a "land ethic" in the private landowner, but he knew this was not enough. As he put it, "Conservation will ultimately boil down to rewarding the private landowner who conserves the public interest." Unfortunately, many Montana sports men and women resist providing such rewards.

Whose Wildlife Is It?

This resistance emanates from the "North American Model of Fish and Wildlife Conservation," which harkens back to colonial times when American colonists asserted that the wildlife belonged to the people rather than the King. The model subjected wildlife to the "rule of capture," meaning the animal belonged to no one until it was possessed by the person who

The great conservationist Aldo Leopold (pictured) believed that private landowners and managers must be compensated for their conservation efforts.

shot or trapped it. The problem is that it can lead to over harvesting known as the "tragedy of the commons."

To prevent this tragedy, fish and game departments were called on to establish and enforce season and bag limits. And, to be sure, these agencies such as the Montana Department of Fish, Wildlife, and Parks did a great deal to restore game to record numbers.

Modern wildlife conservation, however, must go beyond simply setting seasons and bag limits; true conservationists in the tradition of Leopold must find ways of compensating landowners and managers who are stewards of wildlife habitat. The state's "block management program" does this to a degree, but payments are small. Access leases, whether to outfitters or hunters, provide a greater return and link sports people more directly to the landowner.

Oh yes there will be cries from those driving new pickups and pulling ATVs [all terrain vehicles] that this will allow only the rich to hunt. Indeed this will be true of lands providing trophy hunts, but what about the $50 per day access fee for pheasant hunting on a ranch that has fantastic habitat, limits the number of guns, and maintains a sustainable population? This is the type of steward that Leopold had in mind.

Incentives for Landowners

States such as Colorado, New Mexico, and Utah have adopted "ranching for wildlife" programs whereby landowners cooperate with state officials in game and habitat management and allow some public (free) hunting in return for tags to sell at the market price. As a result, landowners in those states have an economic incentive to invest in maintaining fish and wildlife habitat. Those states have added an economic incentive, which encourages more habitat preservation.

Montana sports people must realize that development pressures are forcing ranchers and farmers to squeeze every penny they can from their land. If they rely solely on revenue for wildlife stewardship, hunters and fishers can make it "cows not

U.S. Conservation Banks

When private land is put into a conservation bank, the landowner agrees to manage the land to protect its natural resource values.

1 bank in development for Oregon chub

1 bank (Preble's jumping mouse)

None in Region 3

Interest in banking for timber rattlesnakes in New York

OR

Region 6

Region 1

Region 3

NY

Region 5

VA

1 bank (red-cockaded woodpecker)

CA

CO

At least 30 banks (variety of species and habitats)

AZ

Region 2

Region 4

SC

3 banks (red-cockaded woodpecker)

AL   GA

TX

FL

1 bank (red-cockaded woodpecker)

2 banks for Pima pineapple cactus

4 banks (variety of species and habitats)

1 bank; 1 in development (gopher tortoise)

Interest; no formal banks yet

AK

Region 7

None in Region 7

None in Hawaii

Region 1

Taken from: Stratus Consulting, "A Nationwide Survey of Conservation Banks," prepared for Northwest Fisheries Science Center, December 19, 2003./Northwest Fisheries Science Center, 2003.

condos," as the Montana Land Reliance bumper sticker reads, and add wildlife to the ranching mix.

As you head to the polls, think about access and habitat and about the importance of private property owners in supplying both. Calling for more open access may sound like a panacea, but it ignores the important role of incentives.

Montana's constitution guarantees its citizens a right to "a clean and healthful environment," and private landowners are a crucial supplier of this right. So when you vote, support candidates who promote private property rights, and when you hunt or fish, take time to thank the private landowner.

TWELVE

Hunters Do a Good Job of Managing Wolf Populations

Thomas McIntyre

In the following viewpoint outdoor writer Thomas McIntyre argues that hunters should be allowed to shoot wolves in the Rocky Mountains now that the population has stabilized and the wolf has been taken off the list of animals protected under the Endangered Species Act. A large wolf population means more conflicts between the wolves and livestock, he explains, and without proper management of the wolf population even human lives could be in danger. Hunters have a long history of helping keep wildlife populations in balance, he concludes, and should not be prevented from hunting wolves. McIntyre is the author of several books about hunting, including *The Field & Stream Hunting Optics Handbook,* and has written articles for *Field & Stream, Gray's Sporting Journal,* and *Sports Afield,* for which he is also an editor.

I t was hardly a surprise. On March 28, 2008, the gray wolf in the Northern Rockies was removed from protection under the Endangered Species Act (ESA) and the management of the large predator transferred from the Federal Government to the states of Idaho, Montana, and Wyoming; and some wolves, particularly in

Thomas McIntyre, "Thrown to the Wolves," *Sports Afield,* September 2008. Reproduced by permission.

Wyoming, started to get shot. Within a month of delisting, after vouchsafing to abstain for sixty days from taking any action, a consortium of almost a dozen environmental and animal-rights groups—including the Humane Society of the United States, Defenders of Wildlife, Sierra Club, and Natural Resources Defense Council—filed suit to have the gray wolf re-protected under the ESA. The lawsuit further called for the states to be immediately enjoined from permitting any more wolf kills until the case was settled. (And by the summer of 2008, Federal District Judge Donald W. Malloy of Montana had issued just such a preliminary injunction blocking the removal of the gray wolf in the Northern Rockies from the ESA.)

Ill-Informed Opponents

The sentiment to halt any hunting or killing and as a result any effective management of the wolf has been widespread, as in widespread where the wolves are not. Letters to the editors vowing boycotts of Wyoming over the killing of wolves have appeared in journals hundreds of miles away. In an April 30, 2008, editorial, the increasingly maundering and decreasingly relevant *Los Angeles Times* acknowledged that wolves in the Northern Rockies were "ready for delisting," that "the population exceeded all goals for the [recovery] program," and that "the species should not be kept on a lifeline forever." Therefore, in light of the fact that after March 28th a number of wolves were killed in non-wilderness areas where it was always recognized that their presence would be problematic, and in defiance of the newspaper's own logic, the states were declared, by the *Times*, to have failed to "protect" wolves, and so the U.S. Fish and Wildlife Service [USFWS] should immediately relist the species because it was never "reintroduced to provide target practice for hunters." (The *Times*'s argument was in truth even more insidious, because from out of its, er, hat, the newspaper bandied about a figure of 35 dead wolves since delisting, glaringly omitting to note that while sixteen of those wolves had been taken in Wyoming's controversial "predator" area, four of *those* had been killed by the U.S. Department of

The Northern Rocky Mountain Gray Wolf Recovers

In three recovery areas designated by the federal government, the number of breeding pairs of northern Rocky Mountain gray wolves has increased dramatically.

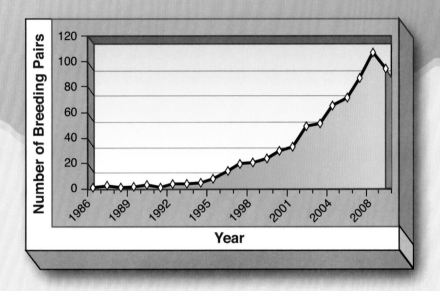

Taken from: U.S. Fish & Wildlife Service, "Rocky Mountain Wolf Recovery 2008 Interagency Annual Report," 2008.

Agriculture Wildlife Services because of livestock conflicts; that some of the other 12 were also taken by ranchers, often with permits, to protect their horses, cattle, or pets; and that the remaining 21 were taken outside of Wyoming altogether, again because of depredation on livestock.)

That was the *Times*'s view at a remove of over eight hundred miles from the wolves of the Northern Rockies. More disturbing perhaps is the way a hunter-conservationist saw the situation at a distance of two thousand miles. John Harrigan writes the "Woods, Water, and Wildlife" column in the *New Hampshire Union Leader*. Over the course of several weeks in April [2008] he made numerous statements in print about wolf delisting, including that it would "give the anti-hunting crowd just the silver bullet they need, and besides, in my book, is just plain wrong"; "wolf-hunting is just the wrong thing, at the wrong time"; and tangentially questioning whether it is even necessary for there to be "science-based" management of the wolves.

This is, to say the least, a rather jaw-dropping attitude to be taken by someone who ought to know something about the dynamics of wildlife populations.

It should be acknowledged, though, that some of the shooters (lets suspend the term "hunters") in Wyoming haven't done much to burnish the image of sportsmen or advance the case for wolf management among the general public since delisting. The *Billings* [MT] *Gazette* reported above the fold on its front page the derring- do of one Wyomingite who "stalked" a wolf for 35 (what is it with this enigmatic number?) miles on the seat of his snow machine, at the end of the pursuit shooting the, one imagines, tongue-lolling animal at 30 yards with his .270. All perfectly legal; and the area where this and other predator wolves have been taken is so inappropriate for the animals because of inevitable run-ins with humans and their animals, that as the head of the USFWS wolf recovery program, Ed Bangs, said in an e-mail, "virtually no packs ever successfully raise young there [or] contribute in a meaningful way to wolf population recovery."

Such human behavior, though, is unlikely to endear average Americans with no experience of wolves or even wolf country to the concept of management.

Admittedly, questions of ethics and public opinion are not inconsequential, just nearly impossible to quantify. What *is* possible to quantify is that the year before delisting, 186 wolves in the Northern Rockies were killed by government agents or under depredation permits or because they posed immediate threats to livestock; and the population *only* continued to increase at the annual rate of nearly 25 percent. This year [2008], delisting or no delisting, that could mean 230-odd wolves might be killed, to which the predator area in Wyoming is likely to contribute only a small fraction; and the population could conceivably expand *another* 25 percent. So in terms of numbers, opposition to wolf management cannot rationally be based on a concern for a possible new extirpation of the wolf in the Northern Rockies; and as a Department of the Interior senior environmental consultant Kate Powers wrote in a commentary in the Greeley, Colorado, *Tribune* [May 18] on the subject of the horrendous decision to list the polar bear under the ESA, "Species are considered 'endangered' under the ESA if they are currently in danger of extinction and are 'threatened' if they are likely to reach endangered status in the foreseeable future," neither of which conditions even remotely applies to the gray wolf at this stage of its recovery.

Good Reasons for Managing Wolves

The reasons for managing wolves are legion, including, ultimately, protection of human life. (William N. Graves's book, *Wolves in Russia: Anxiety Through the Ages*, provides ample evidence for what the risks and consequences, for humans, of *failing* to control wolves can be.) The reason for not managing them is very much singular.

Opposition to sound, scientific management of wolves is opposition to hunting, period. Over a decade ago, when wolf reintroduction in the Northern Rockies began, the most paranoid-sounding claim of wolf opponents was that wild predators were being brought back in order to eliminate the need for licensed hunters to regulate game populations, and so extinguish hunting. Astonishingly, what then seemed an utterly absurd notion manages only to gain credibility with the passage of time.

In its 2007 report on the 2006–2007 winter count of Northern Yellowstone elk, upon which wolves predate heavily, the National Park Service stated that at "the current level of harvest, recreational hunting has very little impact on elk numbers in a population of several thousand animals." More chilling, though, is the next line: "*Hunting has basically been removed as a significant factor regulating Northern Yellowstone elk numbers* [italics mine]." There seems to be a less than subtle suggestion in these words that with wolves now present, hunters need not apply —or hunt. The *Times* in its editorial doesn't even bother with

The author contends that hunters can effectively manage wolf populations, including that of the Northern Rocky Mountain gray wolf (pictured), which was removed from the Endangered Species list in 2008.

couching it in the form of a suggestion: "Protecting livestock is one thing, but hunters have been complaining that the wolves keep down the population of elk, which they would like to hunt themselves. Yet part of the reasoning for reintroducing the wolf was to restore the natural balance in which *animal predators* [again, my italics] kept the populations of elk and deer in check." If that *was* the official reasoning, its pronouncement was studiously obscured at the time of reintroduction.

The first year Montana set a bounty on wolves in 1884, 5,450 pelts were brought in. In 1973 wolves in the Northern Rockies were listed as endangered under the ESA. By 1980, a lone wolf inhabited all of Idaho, Montana, and Wyoming. During 1995–96, an "experimental population" of 66 wolves from Canada was introduced into Yellowstone National Park and central Idaho. And by the time of delisting this year [2008], over 1500 roamed the same region. Yet there are many who refuse to believe that wolf recovery is on the right track. What they also refuse to believe is that, as one of the early backers of wolf introduction, quoted in author Hank Fischer's *Wolf Wars*, said, "Laws don't protect wolves; people protect wolves. Greater protection of wolves is not necessarily achieved through more restrictive laws." Or by throwing hunters—who have had and continue to have one of the most essential roles to play in all wildlife recovery—under the bus. Or to the wolves.

THIRTEEN

Consumers Making Good Choices Can Protect Endangered Fish

Carl Safina and Katherine McLaughlin

In the viewpoint that follows, Carl Safina and Katherine McLaughlin trace the history of sushi, the Japanese delicacy popular in the United States that includes different combinations of seaweed, rice, and raw fish. Many of the fish used in sushi are threatened or endangered, they point out, because of too much consumer demand. Bluefin tuna and octopus should be avoided, they conclude, but an experienced sushi chef will be able to guide consumers to local, tasty alternatives. Safina, who writes frequently about ocean creatures, is a cofounder of the Blue Ocean Institute, where McLaughlin is seafood program director.

A s with all foods, it seems like the more you know about sushi, the more authentic and gentler on the planet your experience can be.

But the story of sushi goes back, way back before sushi was served as raw fish. According to authors Trevor Corson (*The Story of Sushi*) and Hiroko Shimbo (*The Sushi Experience*), sushi dates back to the early centuries A.D., prior to refrigeration, when such preparation techniques were necessary not for impressing your date on a Friday night but for preserving fish. Dur-

Carl Safina and Katherine McLaughlin, "The Evolution of Sushi," *Edible East End*, Winter 2009. Reproduced by permission.

ing the monsoon season, fish made their way from river systems into rice paddies in the inland regions of Southeast Asia (today's Thailand). In order to preserve this important protein source for the drier months, rice farmers would pack the salted and pickled fish with rice, allowing them to ferment.

Like all good stories, sushi's tale has a bit of intrigue: Shimbo points out that it is unknown how or when this type of preserved fish migrated to Japan, though the earliest written references to sushi appear in the eighth century A.D.

Gradually sushi evolved, and in the 14th century the fermentation time was decreased with the use of rice vinegar and rice wine as preserving agents. By the middle of the 19th century, sushi became street food in Edo (today's Tokyo). Just like hot dogs in New York today, pickled fish and rice were assembled on the spot and eaten as a quick bite for the busy city dweller.

You likely wouldn't recognize these ancient iterations of *nigiri*, the simple combination of fish and a hand-formed clump of seasoned rice, as it wasn't until after World War II, when refrigeration and freezing equipment were modernized, that raw fish was served as sushi. Chefs in Los Angeles further transformed this dish and in the 1960s gave it an American twist when they created the California roll.

As any online search for restaurants in America's major cities will reveal, sushi is now widely available in our national cuisine. The NPD Group, a market research firm, calculated that 61 billion restaurant meals were served nationwide last year [2008], and 225 million of them included sushi.

Consider the Source

Where does the future of sushi lie? Consider your own sushi experience. Do you order the same roll every time you treat yourself to this delicacy? Do you consider the geography of your meal and the season?

Sometimes we forget that, in all its exotic grandeur, sushi has an origin beyond the distant shores of Japan. The slices of fish that grace your sashimi plate or balance delicately on the

The Atlantic Bluefin Tuna Is Headed for Collapse

The population of the eastern stock of the Atlantic bluefin tuna (measured by the mass of sexually mature fish) has declined sharply. According to an estimate by the World Wildlife Federation, indicated in red, the stock will disappear by the year 2012.

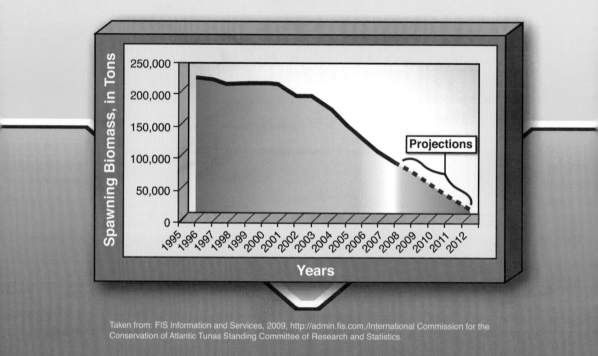

Taken from: FIS Information and Services, 2009, http://admin.fis.com./International Commission for the Conservation of Atlantic Tunas Standing Committee of Research and Statistics.

rice of your *nigiri* came from living creatures in the water. They were born and died and hopefully enjoyed a chance to reproduce somewhere in between.

But there's no need to stash your chopsticks for good, as there are a number of species that you can eat with confidence knowing your seafood was caught or farmed in a way that had minimal impact on fish populations or surrounding habitat.

Though bluefin tuna used to roam the waters just off Long Island in such great schools they reminded me of buffalo on blue prairies, the fishery is all but destroyed by overfishing. Even yellowfin and albacore tuna are now showing signs of depletion in the Atlantic. Striped bass and summer flounder have been locally recruited to do sushi duty for several years. Striped bass (*suzuki*) are a great and local success story, with population numbers rebounded from low levels after strong management was put in place in the 1980s. Summer flounder, locally called fluke, are also recovering due to stringent management and are again common. Both have a mild flavor, making them delicious in *nigiri* or in preparations that include spices.

Pass on *tako*, as octopus populations are declining due to heavy fishing pressure. Instead, try squid (*ika*). Squid can be caught in local waters—Montauk [New York] is one of the nation's largest squid ports—and since they reproduce quickly, this is a sushi dish that can be enjoyed without the side of guilt.

Talk to the Chef

Eating local is a tradition that extends to classical sushi chefs in Japan, according to Shimbo. Rather than ordering the same roll anytime you enjoy sushi, customers there tend to ask the chef what's the fresh catch of the day, and order that.

Try considering new species for your sushi. One place to start is by using a sustainable seafood guide, like the one produced by the Blue Ocean Institute, to learn more about the impact of your fish choices, where your fish comes from or the history and etiquette of eating it.

Talking with your sushi chef is the next step in broadening your sushi horizons. In addition to hearing the story of your sushi—*What port did this fish come in to? Is this fish traditionally eaten in Japan? What is the recommended preparation for this type of fish?*—you can let your chef know if there are species that you would like to try but don't see offered. Perhaps there is a local species that hasn't made its way onto the menu yet because the chef thinks there won't be any demand for the dish. Starting the conversation could help ensure that the story of sushi continues to evolve for millennia to come.

The rise in the worldwide popularity of sushi has threatened or endangered many fish species, according to the authors, who provide tips for choosing sushi selctions that protect endangered fish populations.

Perhaps the next evolution in sushi will involve a sense of time and place and a feeling that your choices are helping ensure teeming oceans.

FOURTEEN

Assisted Migration May Be Some Species' Best Chance for Survival

Michelle Nijhuis

In the following viewpoint Michelle Nijhuis examines the controversy over relocating endangered species when their habitat shrinks or changes. As the global climate becomes warmer, she explains, animals who can easily migrate are moving further north, but some species—including the Florida torreya tree, or *Torreya taxifolia*—cannot migrate quickly enough without human assistance. Although preserving plants and animals in their natural habitat would be best, she concludes, assisted migration may be an important tool for saving some species. Nijhuis is a journalist specializing in science and the environment. In 2006 she won a Science Journalism Award from the American Association for the Advancement of Science.

Torreya State Park perches on the steep, sandy banks of the Apalachicola, where the river twists slowly through the Florida Panhandle toward the Gulf of Mexico. This is one of the most isolated spots in Florida, rich only in plant life and prisons, stupefyingly hot in summer and eerily quiet nearly all year round. Most park visitors are on their way somewhere else, and when Connie Barlow stopped here on a winter day in 1999, she was no exception.

Barlow, trim and now in her fifties, is a writer and naturalist with cropped hair and a childlike air of enthusiasm. She's given to wandering, and back then she shuttled between a trailer in southern New Mexico and an apartment in New York City. That winter, during a detour to Florida, she paused at the park for a look at its raison d'être [reason for being]—an ancient tree species called *Torreya taxifolia*, familiarly known as the Florida torreya or, less romantically, stinking cedar. The park lies at the heart of the tree's tiny range, which stretches little more than twenty miles from the Georgia state line toward the mouth of the Apalachicola. But even at Torreya State Park, Barlow discovered, the Florida torreya is hard to find.

Torreya taxifolia was once a common sight along the Apalachicola, plentiful enough to be cut for Christmas trees, its rot-resistant wood perfect for fence posts. But at some point in the middle of the last century—no one is quite sure when—the trees began to die. Beset by a mysterious disease, overabundant deer, feral hogs, drought, and perhaps a stressful climate, the adult trees were reduced to a handful of mossy trunks, rotting in riverside ravines.

The species persists in Florida as less than a thousand gangly survivors, most only a few feet tall, their trunks no thicker than a child's wrist, none known to reproduce. Much like the American chestnut, these trees are frozen in preadolescence, knocked back by disease or other adversaries before they grow large enough to set seed. To see their grape-sized seeds, Barlow had to visit the state park offices, where two sit preserved in a jam jar.

Barlow continued her travels that winter but returned to the park a few years later. She tracked down some of the few remaining trees and, in a quiet moment, sat under one of the largest specimens, perhaps ten feet tall. The Florida torreya, even at its healthiest, isn't an obviously charismatic tree. Its flat needles are scanty; its trunk lacks the grandeur of a redwood or an old-growth fir; when it does manage to produce seeds, the rotting results smell like vomit. In its diminished state, it inspires more pity than awe; to call its spindly limbs a canopy is a sorry joke.

But when Barlow looked up at the branches of the Florida torreya, she made an impulsive commitment to the species. She'd spent years thinking and writing about evolution and ecology, and was aware of the implications of climate change. She decided the species needed to move north, to cooler, less diseased climes. And since it couldn't move fast enough alone, Barlow would move it herself. . . .

A Controversial Strategy

This is the longstanding conservation credo: With enough space, money, and knowledge, we can protect natural places and, in many cases, restore them by stitching them back together. But while we're welcome to restore, redesign is frowned upon; that sort of tinkering crosses an invisible line between humans and capital-N Nature, and risks making things much worse. We've good reason to distrust ourselves, after all. Until the 1950s, we thought planting kudzu [an invasive Asian vine species] was a good idea.

But climate change calls all this into question. If rising temperatures and changing weather patterns make restoration difficult or impossible, new brands of meddling may sometimes be the only alternative to extinction. Connie Barlow believes *Torreya taxifolia*, with its almost absurdly gloomy prospects in its current range, already requires a new strategy—and she welcomes the chance to provide it.

Barlow describes herself as "more interventionist" than many of the scientists and

The Florida torreya tree, Torreya taxifolia, *has been the subject of controversy surrounding efforts to assist its migration north.*

conservationists she encounters, explaining that her background in ecology and evolutionary biology have immersed her in the long time-scales of evolution. "I don't have a sense of what's normal," she says. "I do have a sense of species moving a lot through time."

Following her first visits to Torreya State Park, Barlow started an e-mail correspondence with botanists, conservationists, and others about the future of the tree. Some, such as paleoecologist Paul Martin, loved the idea of moving *T. taxifolia* north. The Florida torreya is widely believed to be an ice age relict, "left behind" after the last glacial retreat and very possibly better suited for cooler climates, with or without global warming. So why not return it to the southern Appalachians, where it grew during the Pleistocene? These arguments were countered by an ecologist named Mark Schwartz, who has studied the Florida torreya at the Apalachicola Bluffs preserve since the late 1980s, and remains one of the scant handful of scientists with in-depth knowledge of the species. Schwartz defended the chances for restoration in the species' present-day range. Before long, the discussion reached an impasse, and the disagreement found an audience. . . .

The Torreya Guardians

The passionate critics of assisted migration didn't stop Connie Barlow, who moved briskly ahead with her plans for the Florida torreya. She created a website called the Torreya Guardians, where she and a handful of amateur horticulturists began to trade information about *Torreya taxifolia* cultivation in other habitats.

Their vision of the Florida torreya's future begins in the mountains of north Georgia, where the roads narrow and twist, and travel is measured in time instead of distance. Here Jack Johnston, a sleepy-eyed emergency-room nurse and amateur horticulturist, started growing Florida torreya after meeting Connie Barlow at a dinner in North Carolina. On the steep ground behind his house, on terraces that legend has it were

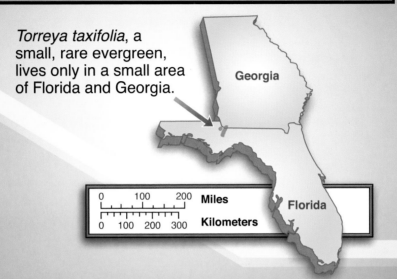

The Current Range of *Torreya Taxifolia*

Torreya taxifolia, a small, rare evergreen, lives only in a small area of Florida and Georgia.

Georgia

Florida

0   100   200   Miles

0   100   200   300   Kilometers

Taken from: Elbert L. Little Jr., *Atlas of United States Trees, vol. 5, Florida.* Washington, DC: U.S. Government Printing Office, 1978; "*Torreya taxifolia,*" The Gymnosperm Database, www.conifers.org/ta/to/taxifolia.htm.

used for growing corn for white lightning in the 1930s, Johnston is cultivating a half-dozen *Torreya taxifolia* seedlings he bought, legally, from a nursery in South Carolina. Each is about two feet high, five years old, and healthy.

Johnston, whose isolated property is full of other rare plants ("I'm moving all sorts of things north," he jokes) is pleased by the apparent flexibility of his charges, and nonchalant about the implications of assisted migration. "People have been moving plants around for a long time," he says. "This idea that we should be territorial about our plants, well, that's just kind of a provincial attitude." . . .

The Debate Expands

In 2007, ecologist Mark Schwartz and two colleagues, Jessica Hellmann and Jason McLachlan, published a paper that modestly proposes a "framework for debate" on assisted migration.

While they criticized "maverick, unsupervised translocation efforts," such as the Torreya Guardians', for their potential to undermine conservation work and create conflict, they directed their harshest criticism at "the far more ubiquitous 'business as usual' scenario that is the current de facto policy." The three scientists take different stands on the notion of assisted migration. All are cautious, but McLachlan is usually the most skeptical, and Hellmann, a University of Notre Dame ecologist who studies butterflies on the northern end of their range in British Columbia, is the most open to the concept. "It's incredibly exciting to think that we could come up with a strategy that might help mitigate the impacts of climate change," she says.

Last fall [2007], to initiate a broader discussion, the three scientists organized a meeting in Davis, California, with other researchers, land managers, environmental groups, and even an environmental ethicist. The Florida torreya isn't the only species that might benefit from immediate assisted migration. The Quino checkerspot butterfly has blinked out on the southern end of its range, in the Mexican state of Baja California, while the northern end of its range, in Southern California, has been transformed by development. In South Africa and Namibia, rising temperatures on the northern edge of the range of the quiver tree are killing the succulent plants before the species has a chance to shift south. . . .

Mark Schwartz, for his part, still holds out hope for the recovery of the Florida torreya in Florida, for a small but healthy population of trees in the shady steephead ravines. But each time he visits the Panhandle, he says, he sees fewer and fewer *Torreya taxifolia*.

FIFTEEN

Protecting Endangered Species Is a Moral Responsibility

Noah Alliance

> The following viewpoint was originally a declaration signed by more than eighty Jewish rabbis and more than thirty Jewish scientists. The viewpoint argues that the Endangered Species Act does important and noble work in protecting and preserving fragile plants and wildlife and that keeping the law strong and effective is in keeping with Jewish belief. Humans are responsible for protecting earth, it contends, and must use their intelligence to make solid decisions based in science. As the biblical figure Noah did, it concludes, humans must save species from extinction. The Noah Alliance, which sponsored the original document, is a collaboration of Jewish, Evangelical, Protestant, and other religious organizations that are concerned about the protection of endangered species and biological diversity.

The passage of the Endangered Species Act thirty-two years ago [in 1973] marked a moment of great human nobility. To save from extinction species identified by scientists as gravely threatened by human activity, the American people provided resources for research, planning, and enforcement to preserve imperiled plants and wildlife and the places they call home. As

Noah Alliance, "The Entirety of Creation," September 2005. www.noahalliance.org. Reproduced by permission.

a result, many of the frailest elements of the North American web of life were spared final destruction and given a chance at rebirth. Of more than 1,800 species under the Endangered Species Act's protections during the past three decades, only nine have been declared extinct—a remarkable record of the Act's positive impact. This represents stewardship in keeping with America's great conservation heritage.

Today, however, the Endangered Species Act is itself endangered by impatience, ideology, and shortsighted, even deceptive, policymaking. Some organizations and members of Congress have been seeking to weaken its habitat protections, hamper the processes of identifying and listing fragile species, politicize what is supposed to be scientific decision-making, and otherwise alter the law in ways that would violate its beneficent vision and set back its accomplishments.

Distinguished voices from diverse communities are forging unique partnerships to prevent such action. Religious leaders and scientists, who may have different visions of how and why the Earth originated, are together affirming a universal moral imperative to protect all life on Earth. And in religious life itself, across traditional and often challenging denominational and ideological boundaries, people of faith are discerning a mandate for stewardship of creation deeply embedded in biblical scripture and commentary.

In this spirit, therefore, and in full agreement with a recent statement by the Academy of Evangelical Scientists and Ethicists, which calls upon religious communities to emulate "the biblical example of Noah as a model for being faithful to God's call to protect endangered species from extinction," we seek here to affirm the Jewish community's longstanding commitment to protect biological diversity. We also affirm our conviction that the Endangered Species Act is one of our generation's richest fulfillments of our biblical destiny as *b'tselem elohim*, created in the image of God (Genesis 1:26), with the unique power and responsibility to shape, preserve, and renew creation through the work of our hands, our hearts, and our minds.

The Bible story of Noah's saving threatened animals, illustrated here, was the inspiration for the formation of the Noah Alliance, a coalition of religious organizations concerned with conservation.

Wonder and Protection

Jewish texts clearly state that all species deserve our wonder and protection. "Of all that the Holy One created in the world, not a single thing is useless," teaches the Talmud (B. Shabbat 77b), while the Midrash (ancient Jewish commentaries on Hebrew scriptures) elaborates, "Even those creatures that you may look upon as superfluous in the world . . . they too are part of the entirety of creation. The Holy One effects purpose through all creatures, even through a snake, a scorpion, a gnat, a frog" (Genesis Rabbah 10:7). Every species of plant or animal is thus understood by Jewish tradition to occupy an ecological niche in our interdependent, living world.

Furthermore, Jewish tradition puts preservation of the environment squarely on our shoulders. "Do not spoil My world, for if you do, there is nobody to fix it after you" (Kohelet Rabbah 7:13).

Today, in a time of marvelous innovation and discovery, science has given the ancient environmental wisdom of Judaism new strength and meaning. Genetics, ecology, taxonomy, medicine, and other sciences all indicate that life is an interconnected web whose diversity of species is an irreplaceable boon to human health and well-being. Gene research and genome mappings have shown how every creature and plant carries within it a life-urge that is eons older than any scripture. The ongoing discovery of new species, and those rare instances when we learn that species we thought extinct cling to survival, point to the strength of the life-urge and its capacity for renewal—if we humans will only seek to transcend our baser natures and rise to our religious, ethical, and legal responsibilities of stewardship, both individually and collectively. But, as noted by the Ecological Society of America, a professional society representing more than 8,000 scientists around the world, "The loss of biological diversity that we are currently observing is unprecedented."

The Guidance of Religion and Science

Two great disciplines, religion and science, have pointed us in the direction of universal values and wise policy. Science points the way with trail markers of objectivity and understanding. Religion then offers tools with which to discipline ourselves to put aside greed, self-deceit, and narrow self-interest, and to embrace, instead, the profound responsibilities assigned to us as the guardians of creation. Rabbi Elijah Gaon, the 18th-century sage of Vilna, taught that: "Torah and science are intertwined." The Jewish people have a long, proud history of fulfilling his teaching—as inno-

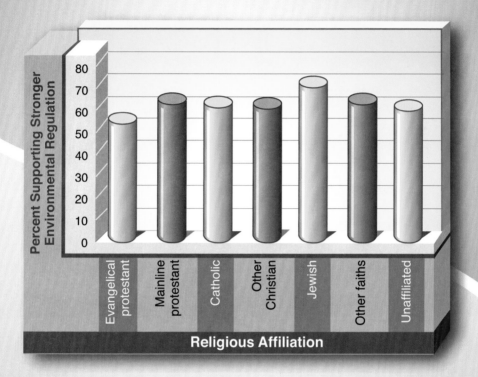

Religion and Environmental Concern

In a 2004 survey sponsored by the Pew Forum on Religion & Public Life, more than half of the respondents indicated that they favored stronger environmental regulation.

Percent Supporting Stronger Environmental Regulation

80
70
60
50
40
30
20
10
0

Evangelical protestant
Mainline protestant
Catholic
Other Christian
Jewish
Other faiths
Unaffiliated

Religious Affiliation

Taken from: Pew Forum on Religion & Public Life, 2004. http://pewforum.org/docs/?DocID=121.

vators in the scientific community and as believers in science as a pathway to human dignity.

We are particularly disturbed, therefore, by criticisms of the Endangered Species Act that undermine the role of science in environmental decision-making. Recent legislative initiatives and policy reports have distorted statistics, used unrealistic timetables, questioned the integrity of scientists, and couched themselves in pseudo-scientific language in ways that amount to what the Jewish tradition calls *g'neivat da'at*, stealing the mind.

We urge instead that discussion of the Endangered Species Act's ongoing relationship to species recovery, land use, economic development, political ideology, and other concerns be conducted as "controversy for the sake of heaven," which the Jewish tradition describes as having "lasting value" (Pirke Avot 5:19). Surely the goals of the Endangered Species Act are goals "for the sake of heaven," with value that stretches deep into our past and holds profound promise for our future. In July 2004, more than 400 members of the scientific community wrote members of Congress, expressing "serious unease with proposals in Congress that may undermine the integrity of science and thus further distort or hamper endangered species conservation decisions."

We call upon U.S. policymakers to emulate the forethought, self-restraint, and prodigious effort modeled by the biblical Noah—"a righteous man . . . blameless in his age" (Genesis 6:9). While the Bible says little about the actual labors that Noah and his family endured to save Earth's countless species from the floods of extinction, the 16th-century *Midrash Tanhuma* portrays him as a man of foresight who planted and cultivated cedar trees over the course of a century—all the while planning the construction of his cedarwood ark and withstanding the mockery of his neighbors.

To us, the Endangered Species Act is the legislative equivalent of Noah's cedar grove. We are determined, with our allies in other faith communities, to see it maintained and strengthened as a resource for building our environmental future.

What You Should Know About Endangered Species

Endangered Species in the United States

According to the U.S. Fish and Wildlife Service, as of November 5, 2009:

- A total of 1,361 U.S. species are listed as threatened or endangered; 614 animal species and 747 plant species are listed.
- Another sixty-four U.S. species have been officially proposed in the Federal Register for listing as threatened or endangered: eighteen animal species and forty-six plant species.
- Government agencies have enough information on file to support official proposals for listing 248 more species: 138 animal species are candidates for listing, along with 111 plant species.
- The states with the highest number of threatened and endangered species are Hawaii (330), California (309), Alabama (117), Florida (115), and Texas (94).
- The states with the smallest number of threatened and endangered species are North Dakota (10), Vermont (11), South Dakota (12), Alaska (14), Montana (14), and New Hampshire (14). The District of Columbia has 7.

A 2007 report from the National Wildlife Federation, *Fair Funding for Wildlife*, reports several successes in efforts to protect species under the Endangered Species Act:

- Only about 500 breeding pairs of the American bald eagle were left in the lower forty-eight United States in the 1960s; more than 7,000 pairs exist today.

- In the middle of the twentieth century, only a few hundred gray wolves lived in the lower forty-eight states; today they number 3,500 or more, with 2,500 in Minnesota, 500 in Wisconsin, and 500 individuals in western states.
- Although grizzly bear habitat has declined, protected habitats like that in Yellowstone National Park provide homes for some grizzlies. Their population in Yellowstone has increased from fewer than 250 in 1975 to more than 600 today.
- Efforts to protect the peregrine falcon under the Endangered Species Act were so successful that the bird was taken off the threatened and endangered list in 1999.
- The National Wildlife Federation estimated fully funding the Endangered Species Act would cost approximately $478 million in 2008—about the cost of one cup of coffee per American per year.

In a January 2009 poll conducted by the Pew Research Center for People and the Press, respondents were asked to identify which of twenty national issues should be considered top domestic priorities for the president and Congress:

- The highest-ranked issue was the economy; 85 percent of the respondents ranked the economy as a "top priority." Jobs was chosen by 82 percent, terrorism by 76 percent, health care by 59 percent, and the environment by only 41 percent.
- In 2008 strengthening the nation's economy was chosen by 75 percent of the respondents; protecting the environment was chosen by 56 percent.
- Whether a respondent considers protecting the environment as a "top priority" is not strongly influenced by gender. In the 2009 survey, 43 percent of women and 39 percent of men ranked the environment as a top priority. In January 2008 the numbers were 57 percent of women and 55 percent of men.

Endangered Species Around the World

As reported in a 2009 update to the International Union for Conservation of Nature (IUCN):

- Of the 47,677 species that conservations have assessed, 17,291 are in danger of becoming extinct.

- Twenty-one percent of all known mammals are under threat, along with 30 percent of all known amphibians and 12 percent of all known birds, as well as 28 percent of the reptiles, 37 percent of the freshwater fish, 70 percent of the plants, and 35 percent of the invertebrates assessed so far.
- Amphibians are the group of species most severely threatened. Of the 6,285 known species, 1,895 are in danger of extinction. Of these, 39 are already extinct or living only in captivity, 484 are critically endangered, 754 are endangered, and 657 are vulnerable.
- Of the world's 5,490 mammals, 79 are extinct or live only in captivity, 188 are critically endangered, 449 are endangered, and 505 are vulnerable.
- Reptiles account for 1,677 species on the IUCN Red List. Many species of reptiles have not yet been studied and counted, but 293 reptile species were added to the list in 2009.
- Of the 1,677 species, 469 are threatened with extinction, and 22 are already extinct or live only in captivity.
- Of the 12,151 plants on the IUCN Red List, 8,500 are threatened with extinction, with 114 already extinct or extinct in the wild.
- Of the 47,677 species assessed, 19,023 species are labeled as "of least concern." Data for categorizing 6,557 species is still insufficient.

Among the nearly extinct species are:
- The Amur leopard, native to the far eastern regions of Russia. The National Geographic Society estimates that only twenty-five to thirty-four remain.
- The hen harrier, a bird of prey that lives in Great Britain. Natural England and the Royal Society for the Protection of Birds report that only six pairs bred young birds in 2009, down from ten in 2008.
- The Saola, a species of wild Asian cattle. The international Saolo Working Group estimates that only 250 adults remain, with the population decreasing rapidly. The existence of the reclusive Saolo, whose Latin name is *Pseudoryx nghetinhensis*, was not discovered until 1993.

- The tropical clownfish, featured in the movie *Finding Nemo*. Billy Sinclair, senior lecturer at the Cumbria University in Australia, reports that the average school of clownfish near Queensland, Australia, has shrunk from twenty-five fish to only six. About half of the tropical clownfish kept in aquariums are caught in the ocean; the rest are bred for sale in captivity.
- The Iberian lynx, which lives in central and southern Spain. The group S.O.S. Lynx estimates that only 100 to 150 remain.
- The Javan rhino, of the island of Java, whose horn is valuable for making Chinese medicine. A few Javan rhinos live in zoos in Java and Vietnam, but fewer than sixty of the animals remain in the world, according to the IUCN.
- The South China tiger. According to the World Wildlife Fund, the tiger has not been seen in the wild for about twenty years, and approximately sixty live in zoos and wildlife parks.

What You Should Do About Endangered Species

Because so many of the most famous endangered plants and animals —polar bears, pandas, baobob trees, marine turtles, and tigers— live far away, it might seem that there is not much you can do to help protect endangered species. It is true that governments will have to take some of the important steps necessary to preserve habitats, prevent poaching and smuggling, and combat pollution and global warming. But even your own neighborhood may be home to a little-known species in trouble, and actions you take at home and in your community can make a big difference.

What an Individual Can Do

Many species are threatened or endangered because pollution has made it impossible for them to live in their preferred habitats. And every bit of pollution contributes to the problem. Think about a few drops of nail polish remover or paint thinner sent down the bathroom drain and eventually reaching rivers and streams—and then think about what could happen if every one of the more than 100 million homes in the United States put just a few drops down the drain. Get in the habit of disposing of hazardous materials properly. You can learn more about disposing of household wastes from the Environmental Protection Agency (www.epa.gov).

Many homes use hazardous materials unnecessarily; check your basement or garage, and ask the adults in your home if you could help them find safer alternatives to the pesticides, herbicides, and cleaning products they buy. Composting in the backyard or even in containers can be a good alternative to chemical fertilizers.

An easy way to reduce the pollution you create is to avoid wasting electricity, which is typically generated from pollution-producing coal-fired plants. Turn off lights, televisions, and computers when you are not using them. Unplug your chargers when your phone and MP3 player are charged. And do not waste water. Take shorter showers, and turn off the water while you are brushing your teeth. Clean water is a precious resource, and many species depend on it for survival.

The U.S. Fish and Wildlife Service reports that keeping your cat indoors will help protect the species that cats naturally hunt—birds, mice, lizards, and other animals. House cats are domesticated animals, and they do not need to hunt to survive. The agency suggests that if you cannot keep your cat inside, it would be helpful to put a small bell around its neck to warn animals before the cat gets too near.

Once your cat is safely indoors or belled, set up a bird-feeding station and a bird bath—a better use of that fresh water you are saving. Plant flowers that attract and feed butterflies. If you live on a large piece of land, encourage your family to leave old trees standing to provide nesting areas for animals, and leave some areas of bushes and shrubs untended. The National Wildlife Federation offers tips through its Backyard Wildlife Habitat program (www.nwf.org/backyardwildlifehabitat).

The Importance of Working in Groups

Probably a group in your area is dedicated to protecting wildlife. It might be a chapter of national groups like the Audubon Society, the Nature Conservancy, or Ducks Unlimited, or your state's Department of Natural Resources. Your school might even have a nature or environmental club. Working together, people can tackle larger projects. The Nature Conservancy (www.nature.org), for example, organizes occasional "work days," when volunteers and Conservancy staff spend a day removing invasive species so native plants can flourish. For more than one hundred years, the National Audubon Society has sponsored an annual Christmas Bird Count, a three-week period when tens of thousands of volunteers across the country head outside with binoculars and bird lists to record how many birds of which species they see. Local groups and schools plant native trees on eroding river banks

National parks and national wildlife refuges provide important habitat for endangered species—and important opportunities for people to see them in the wild. Many of these areas, along with conservation centers and rescue centers, provide opportunities for volunteers to help with grooming trails, cleaning and building cages and nesting boxes, or feeding and monitoring animals.

When you visit these areas, take the rules seriously. These rules have been established by experts in conservation to help prevent visitors from accidentally damaging habitat or threatening plants and animals. Always follow fire regulations, and never litter. Do not bring your dogs or other pets to visit threatened wildlife habitats. And no matter how tempting, do not pick flowers or other plants, and do not gather eggs, seeds, or rocks. In the same way, be sure you know and follow hunting and fishing regulations, which are designed to ensure that animals are taken in the right numbers to achieve healthy populations.

One of the most important things groups of individuals can do is make their voices heard by those who have the most power to make big changes. A school club can write letters to local representatives or city officials—or even arrange to speak at a city commission meeting or on the local radio station—to remind officials about the importance of preserving habitat. You might consider getting your school or town to plant trees or gardens in honor of Arbor Day (the last Friday in April) or Earth Day (April 22). Encourage your town to learn about becoming a Tree City USA, and work toward earning the certification.

On a larger scale, national activist groups combine their voices to influence members of Congress to pass legislation that protects endangered species. They need volunteers to help with research on environmental issues, prepare educational materials, and participate in events and fund-raising.

While you are still in school, take advantage of formal opportunities to learn about the world and the species that live in it. Consider whether you would enjoy a career as a conservation officer, biologist, ranger, activist, or legislator helping to protect endangered species. The U.S. Fish and Wildlife Service publishes information about conservation careers at http://library .fws.gov/Pubs9/careers_5-2000.pdf.

ORGANIZATIONS TO CONTACT

The editors have compiled the following list of organizations concerned with the issues debated in this book. The descriptions are derived from materials provided by the organizations. All have publications or information available for interested readers. The list was compiled on the date of publication of the present volume; the information provided here may change. Be aware that many organizations take several weeks or longer to respond to inquiries, so allow as much time as possible for the receipt of requested materials.

Conservation International
2011 Crystal Dr., Ste. 500, Arlington, VA 22202
(703) 341-2400 or (800) 429-5660
Web site: www.conservation.org

Conservation International is an organization of scientists, field staff, and policy experts working to empower societies to responsibly and sustainably care for nature for the well-being of humanity. The Center for Applied Biodiversity Science (CABS) is Conservation International's hub of scientific research. The Center's world-renowned scientists develop the tools required to protect earth's biodiversity and ensure that conservation action is based on sound, reliable, and verifiable science. The organization's Web site features an interactive digital magazine, *Team Earth*, a monthly e-newsletter, RSS feeds, photos, videos, as well as podcasts, ring tones, and screen savers.

Defenders of Wildlife
1130 Seventeenth St. NW, Washington, DC 20036
(800) 385-9712
e-mail: defenders@mail.defenders.org
Web site: www.defenders.org

Founded in 1947 as the Defenders of Furbearers, Defenders of Wildlife is a group of scientists, attorneys, and teachers supported by half a million members dedicated to preserving North America's native wildlife species and habitats. The group publishes *Defenders* magazine and issues news releases, electronic newsletters, and reports, including *Livestock and Wolves*. Its Web site also features a blog, a children's section, fact sheets, and computer wallpapers.

Ducks Unlimited
One Waterfowl Way, Memphis, TN 38120
(800) 453-8257 or (901) 758-3825
Web site: www.ducks.org

Ducks Unlimited is the world's leader in wetlands and waterfowl conservation. It was founded in 1937 by a small group of hunters and conservationists working to protect wetland waterfowl habitats in the United States and Canada. Valuing the sport and the heritage of hunting, the group works to conserve waterfowl and wetlands, to encourage its members to practice ethical treatment of species and land, and to make science-based policy decisions. The group produces *Ducks Unlimited* magazine, a newsletter, a television series on the Outdoor Channel, videos, and a photo gallery.

Endangered Species Coalition
PO Box 65195, Washington, DC 20035
(240) 353-2765
Web site: www.stopextinction.org

The Endangered Species Coalition is a national network of hundreds of conservation, scientific, education, religious, sporting, outdoor recreation, business, and community organizations working to protect our nation's disappearing wildlife and last remaining wild places. Through education, outreach, and citizen involvement, it works to protect endangered species and the special places where they live. The coalition's Web site offers interactive maps, press releases, a "Stop Extinction" blog, action alerts, and materials about the Endangered Species Act.

Greenpeace
702 H St. NW, Ste. 300, Washington, DC 20001
(202) 462-1177
e-mail: info@wdc.greenpeace.org
Web site: www.greenpeace.org/usa

Greenpeace is an independent nonprofit organization with chapters around the world. Founded in 1971, it focuses on worldwide threats to the planet's biodiversity and environment, including oceans and forests. The group calls attention to its mission through public acts of nonviolent civil disobedience. Greenpeace issues news releases, videos, and reports, including *Carting Away the Oceans*, *Canned Tuna's Hidden Catch*, and *Slaughtering the Amazon*.

National Audubon Society
225 Varick St., 7th Fl., New York, NY 10014
(212) 979-3000
Web site: www.audubon.org

Incorporated in 1905, the National Audubon Society works to conserve and restore natural ecosystems, focusing on birds, other wildlife, and their habitats for the benefit of humanity and the earth's biological diversity. Its more than five hundred local chapters operate community-based nature centers and chapters, scientific and educational programs, and advocacy on behalf of areas sustaining important bird populations. The organization publishes *Audubon* magazine, and its Web site offers articles, illustrations, puzzles, games, and teaching materials.

National Center for Public Policy Research
501 Capitol Ct. NE, Washington, DC 20002
(202) 543-4110
e-mail: info@nationalcenter.org
Web site: www.nationalcenter.org

The National Center for Public Policy Research, founded in 1982, is a communications and research foundation dedicated to providing free market solutions to today's public policy problems. Its

Center for Environmental and Regulatory Affairs focuses on endangered species, forest policy, fuel economy, global warming, invasive species, nuclear policy, property rights, and smart growth. Its Web site offers news releases, a blog about endangered species, *National Policy Analysis* reports, and a polar bear information center that includes a video entitled *Don't Trust the Polar Bear: A Parody Ad.*

Natural Resources Defense Council (NRDC)
40 W. Twentieth St., New York, NY 10011
(212) 727-2700
e-mail: nrdcinfo@nrdc.org
Web site: www.nrdc.org

The NRDC works to protect wildlife and wild places and to ensure a healthy environment for all life on earth. The council is an environmental action organization that supports pro-environmental legislation. Specifically, it calls on government to work with its citizens to protect endangered species, reduce pollution, and create a sustainable way of life for humankind. Recent projects have focused on whales, grizzly bears, wolves, and protecting the Endangered Species Act. The group publishes a quarterly magazine, *OnEarth*, and e-mail bulletins, including *Earth Action*, *Legislative Watch*, and *This Green Life*.

Noah Alliance
(707) 826-1948
Web site: www.noahalliance.org

The Noah Alliance is a collaboration of Jewish, Evangelical, Protestant, and other religious community organizations and individual people of faith concerned about the protection of endangered species and biological diversity. Members include Restoring Eden, Coalition on the Environment and Jewish Life, and the Academy of Evangelical Scientists and Ethicists. The Noah Alliance gathers written materials pertaining to conservation from a faith perspective, with an emphasis on the protection of endangered species and the web of life, and makes these materials available through its Web site. Materials include sample sermons and sermon tips, songs, study guides, articles, essays, lectures, and faith community statements.

Oceana
1350 Connecticut Ave. NW, 5th Fl., Washington, DC 20036
(202) 833-3900 or (877) 762-3262
e-mail: info@oceana.org
Web site: http://na.oceana.org

Oceana, which seeks to make our oceans as rich, healthy, and abundant as they once were, was founded in 2001 by a group of charitable foundations. The organization works internationally to alleviate overfishing, ocean acidification, and habitat destruction problems through policy-oriented campaigns. Its Web site features a blog, a newsletter, tips, and recipes for responsible seafood eating, a list of green grocers, and scientific reports, including *Hungry Oceans: What Happens When the Prey Is Gone?* and *As Goes the Arctic, So Goes the Planet.*

The Pew Environment Group
1200 Eighteenth St. NW, 5th Fl., Washington, DC 20036
(202) 887-8800
e-mail: info@pewtrusts.org
Web site: www.pewtrusts.org

One of the nation's largest environmental scientific and advocacy organizations, the Pew Environment Group is a major force in educating the public and policy makers about the causes, consequences, and solutions to environmental problems. Pew is a nonprofit, nonpartisan organization creating educational programs that focus on protecting ocean life, wilderness protection and public lands, and global warming. It issues news releases, electronic newsletters, e-alerts, and scientific reports through its main Web site and sponsors issue-specific Web sites, including www.endoverfishing.org.

Property and Environmental Research Center (PERC)
2048 Analysis Dr., Ste. A, Bozeman, MT 59718

(406) 587-9591
e-mail: perc@perc.org
Web site: www.perc.org

PERC, the nation's oldest and largest institute dedicated to improving environmental quality through markets and property rights, pioneered the approach known as free market environmentalism. Research is at the heart of the center's work, followed by outreach and education. Its Web site has an extensive library of articles, books, reports, opinion columns, and guides, with titles including "Lessons from Fisheries Reform," "Hunting for Habitat," and "Lessons from British Columbia: Public Forest Management." The group also publishes the quarterly magazine *PERC Reports*.

U.S. Fish and Wildlife Service
1849 C St. NW, Washington, DC 20240
(800) 344-9453
Web site: www.fws.gov

Created by Congress in 1871, the U.S. Fish and Wildlife Service works "to conserve, protect and enhance fish, wildlife, and plants and their habitats for the continuing benefit of the American people." The agency studies species and their habitats, awards grant funding for scientific investigations, enforces the Endangered Species Act (ESA), and manages the federal Duck Stamp conservation program. Its Web site features the quarterly *Endangered Species Bulletin*, brochures about the ESA, information for landowners, fact sheets about particular species, posters, a slide show, and material for students and teachers.

U.S. Sportsmen's Alliance (USSA)
801 Kingsmill Pkwy., Columbus, OH 43229
(614) 888-4868
e-mail: info@ussportsmen.org
Web site: www.ussportsmen.org

The USSA works to protect and advance the rights of hunters, trappers, anglers, and scientific wildlife management professionals.

The alliance combats the attacks made on America's sportsman traditions by antihunting and animal rights extremists through coalition building, ballot issue campaigning, and legislative and government relations. Its Web site features the monthly electronic magazine *Sentry*, archived back issues of the *Bear Hunter Rights Quarterly*, action alerts, state and federal reports, and a "bill tracker," analyzing proposed legislation currently working its way through Congress.

BIBLIOGRAPHY

Books

Terry Lee Anderson and Peter Jensen Hill, *The Not So Wild, Wild West: Property Rights on the Frontier*. Stanford, CA: Stanford University Press, 2004.

Anthony Barnosky, *Heatstroke: Nature in an Age of Global Warming*. Washington, DC: Island/Shearwater, 2009.

Jeff Corwin, *100 Heartbeats: The Race to Save Earth's Most Endangered Species*. Emmaus, PA: Rodale, 2009.

Peter Ellis, *Tuna: A Love Story*. New York: Knopf, 2008.

Richard Ellis, *On Thin Ice*. New York: Knopf, 2009.

Terry Glavin, *The Sixth Extinction: Journey Among the Lost and Left Behind*. New York: St. Martin's, 2007.

Dale Goble and J. Scott Michael, *The Endangered Species Act at Thirty*. Washington, DC: Island, 2006.

Jane Goodall, Thane Maynard, and Gail E. Hudson, *Hope for Animals and Their World: How Endangered Species Are Being Rescued from the Brink*. New York: Grand Central, 2009.

Roger S. Gottlieb, *A Greener Faith: Religious Environmentalism and Our Planet's Future*. New York: Oxford University Press, 2006.

Will Graves, *Wolves in Russia: Anxiety Through the Ages*. Calgary, AB: Temeron, 2007.

Richard Mackay, *The Atlas of Endangered Species*. Berkeley: University of California Press, 2009.

Sean McDonagh, *The Death of Life: The Horror of Extinction*. Dublin: Columba Press, 2004.

George McGavin, *Endangered: Wildlife on the Brink of Extinction*. Buffalo, NY: Firefly, 2006.

Gary Paul Nabhan and Ashley Rood, *Renewing America's Food Traditions: Saving and Savoring the Continent's Most Endangered Foods*. White River Junction, VT: Chelsea Green, 2008.

Laurel Adams Neme, *Animal Investigators: How the World's First Wildlife Forensics Lab Is Solving Crimes and Saving Endangered Species*. New York: Scribner, 2009.

Carl Safina, *Voyage of the Turtle: In Pursuit of the World's Last Dinosaur*. New York: Holt, 2006.

Bridget Joan Stutchbury, *Silence of the Songbirds*. New York: Walker, 2007.

Malcolm Tait, *Going, Going, Gone? Animals and Plants on the Brink of Extinction and How You Can Help*. London: Think, 2006.

Robert Traer, *Doing Environmental Ethics*. Boulder, CO: Westview, 2009.

Cat Urbigit, *Yellowstone Wolves: A Chronicle of the Animal, the People, and the Politics*. Blacksburg, VA: McDonald and Woodward, 2008.

Peter D. Ward, *Under a Green Sky: Global Warming, the Mass Extinctions of the Past, and What They Can Tell Us About Our Future*. New York: HarperCollins, 2007.

David Samuel Wilcove, *No Way Home: The Decline of the World's Great Animal Migrations*. Island/Shearwater, 2008.

Periodicals

Jerry Adler, "The Race for Survival," *Newsweek*, June 9, 2008.

Peter Alsop, "The Last Days of Fish," *Good Magazine*, September/October 2008.

Ben Block, "Global Bird Species in Serious Decline," *World Watch*, September/October 2009.

Jennifer Bogo, "Fighting the Current: Can North America's Biggest, Oldest Salamander Survive Changing Times?" *National Parks*, Spring 2009.

Colin Campbell and Kate Lunau, "The War over the Polar Bear: Who's Telling the Truth About the Fate of a Canadian Icon?" *Maclean's*, February 4, 2008.

Juliet Eilperin, "Major Decline Found in Some Bird Groups: But Conservation Has Helped Others," *Washington Post*, March 20, 2009.

David A. Fahrenthold, "Saving Species No Longer a Beauty Contest: Homely Creatures Receiving More Help," *Washington Post*, June 29, 2009.

Cynthia Graber, "The Sea Has Eyes," *Boston Globe Magazine*, July 12, 2009.

Alex Halperin, "Cat Fight: The Foreclosure Crisis Has Walloped Florida's Gulf Coast, but Sprawl Still Threatens the State's Endangered Panther," *Earth Island Journal*, Autumn 2009.

H. Josef Hebert, "U.S. Jaguar Plan Foiled by Border Fence, Critics Say," *National Geographic*, January 18, 2008.

Jane Kay, "Overfishing Imperils Ocean Life, Study Says," *San Francisco Chronicle*, March 3, 2009.

Wayne Lynch, "Does Anyone Give a Hoot?" *Canadian Wildlife*, March/April 2008.

Jessica Marshall, "U.S.-Mexico Border Fence May Snag Wildlife," *Discovery News*, July 8, 2009.

Erin McCarthy, "Welcome to the Food Chain: The Good News: Once-Endangered Predators Are Making a Comeback. The Bad News: Their Favorite Habitat Might Be in Your Backyard," *Popular Mechanics*, July 2009.

Colin Nickerson, "The Great Woodpecker Hunt," *Boston Globe*, February 10, 2008.

Devin Nunes, "It's Fish Versus Farmers in the San Joaquin Valley," *Wall Street Journal*, August 15, 2009.

Elizabeth Quill, "Species in Trouble: Many Mammals, Corals Face Extinction," *Science News*, January 9, 2009.

Kirk Repanshek, "Leap Frog: An Endangered Amphibian Is Making a Comeback, One Lake at a Time," *Audubon*, September/October 2009.

Ian Sample, "Wildlife Extinction Rates 'Seriously Underestimated,'" *Guardian*, July 2, 2008.

M. David Stirling, "Blame 'Shortage' on Misguided Environmentalists," *Sacramento Bee*, June 14, 2009.

Bryan Walsh, "The New Age of Extinction," *Time*, April 13, 2009.

Jennifer Weeks, "Saving the Blue Iguana," *National Geographic Kids*, February 2009.

Matt Weiser, "Huge Hurdles Ahead for Effort to Restore Fisheries," *Sacramento Bee*, June 22, 2009.

Jennifer Winger, "The Last Bison," *Nature Conservancy*, Winter 2008.

———, "Jaguar," *Nature Conservancy*, Spring 2009.

Deborah Zabarenko, "Menaces to Oceans: CO_2, Plastic Bags, Overfishing," *Reuters*, June 8, 2009.

Yvette Zandbergen, "A Garden Under Siege: Rare Plants in Ontario's Unique Walpole Island Ecosystem Face Threats from All Sides," *Canadian Wildlife*, November/December 2008.

INDEX

PICTURE CREDITS